Explorations at Sodom

TWO EXPLORERS
IN THE LAND
OF SODOM

Explorations at Sodom

THE STORY OF ANCIENT SODOM IN THE
LIGHT OF MODERN RESEARCH

By
MELVIN GROVE KYLE, D.D., LL.D.

Author of "The Deciding Voice of the Monuments," "The Problem of the Pentateuch," "Moses and the Monuments," etc.

ILLUSTRATED

Eugene, Oregon

Wipf and Stock Publishers
199 W 8th Ave, Suite 3
Eugene, OR 97401

Explorations at Sodom
The Story of Ancient Sodom in the Light of Modern Research
By Kyle, Melvin Grove
ISBN 13: 978-1-55635-450-2
ISBN 10: 1-55635-450-9
Publication date 5/1/2007
Previously published by Fleming Revell, 1927

PREFACE

THE story of Sodom and Gomorrah has been jeered at by unbelievers only less than that of Jonah and the whale. The story of Jonah and the whale has perhaps suffered from the popular unreliability of fish stories. Moreover, it does not admit of scientific investigation. That particular "great fish" cannot be produced, nor the logbook of his voyage examined, nor the records of the custom house—which might show what kind of cargo he delivered at Joppa.

With the story of Sodom and Gomorrah it is very different—such natural materials as have a place in the story do not go out of existence, such catastrophes leave remains, and remains do not move around. In fact, all these things have now been carefully examined by scientific investigators. This book tells the story.

Now, the telling of the story needs only this word of introduction. I conceive the popular telling of dry-as-dust facts on a recondite subject to be one of the greatest services a writer may render. That service I endeavour to render here. There is needed only this final touch of realism, that I should make known that these letters from Sodom are real letters. *"En route,"* "Kir of Moab," "Camp Wady Numeirah," "Camp Ghor-es-Safieh," and even "the Shade of the Thorn-tree" and the "Deck of the Motor-boat," are real places at which the materials were prepared.

It only remains to give credit to the *Sunday School Times*, the *Bibliotheca Sacra*, the *Annals of the Victoria Institute* and *American School of Oriental Research at Jerusalem*, in which this material was first published, and then to tell the story of ancient Sodom in the light of modern science.

M. G. K.

Xenia Theological Seminary,
Saint Louis, Missouri.

CONTENTS

I. PITCHING OUR TENTS TOWARD SODOM - 11
  Letter One: *En Route to Bible Lands*
  Letter Two: *Latin Parish House, Kerak, Moab*
  Letter Three: *At Camp in Henzireh, Moab*
  Letter Four: *Camp Wady Numeirah*
  Letter Five: *Camp at Ghor-Es-Safieh, Moab*
  Letter Six: *Camp at Ghor-El-Mezra'ah, Moab*

II. CIVILIZATION IN THE JORDAN VALLEY   81
  Letter Seven: *In the Shade of a Thorn-Tree, at Sodom*

III. A TRAGIC STORY IN HISTORY AND PROPHECY - - - - - - - 100
  Letter Eight: *In the Shade of a Thorn-Tree, at Sodom*

IV. UNSCIENTIFIC SPECULATIONS OF PILGRIMS AND TRAVELLERS - - - - - 107
  Letter Nine: *Under the Same Thorn-Tree*

V. THE STORY OF ANCIENT SODOM IN THE LIGHT OF MODERN SCIENCE - - - 122
  Letter Ten: *On the Dead Sea*

VI. CONCLUSION - - - - - - 139
  Letter Eleven: *The Port of Jericho*

ILLUSTRATIONS

Facing Page

TWO EXPLORERS IN THE LAND OF SODOM - Title

RUINS OF FORTRESS ERECTED TO PROTECT THE
GREAT HIGH PLACE - - - - - 40

A GREAT GORGE IN THE MOUNTAINS OF MOAB - 84

I

PITCHING OUR TENTS TOWARD SODOM

LETTER ONE:
EN ROUTE TO BIBLE LANDS

THE fascination of the horrible seems irresistible. The announcement of a proposed expedition to Sodom and Gomorrah, Cities of the Plain, made by *The Sunday School Times* and, a little later, through the Associated Press, aroused a widespread interest.

The announcement brought letters from a flood of aspirants for a trip to Palestine, aspirants of every kind, from porters to artists. Most of them desired only "reasonable compensation" and travelling expenses. As the archaeologists received neither travelling expenses nor "reasonable compensation," these requests evoked, I fear, a disappointing answer.

Urgent request also for some announcement of what we were "going to find" provoked a smile, a subtle scientific smile, but, considering its earnestness, the request however unscientific, could not be entirely ignored. So I ventured upon a summary of what has been known about the Cities of the Plain, but with this caveat, that what we know, or do not know, of the Cities of the Plain is exceedingly interesting now, ere we set out in search of new and accurate knowledge on the subject; we can only hope that what we now think we know may not be amusing after we learn the exact facts. That summary, both corrected and expanded by facts newly discovered, will find more appropriate place in a later one of these letters.

We had a longer journey to the starting-point than had Abraham and Lot at Bethel whence Lot "pitched *his* tent toward Sodom." We not only "went up out of Egypt" as did they, but crossed an ocean, and a continent, and the Great Sea.

Lot's career gave a bad reputation to the idea of pitching one's tent toward Sodom; it is hoped that no such lamentable experience as that of Lot awaits the expedition of Xenia Theological Seminary as we pitch our tents toward Sodom. Lot made his experience to mean facing toward moral disaster; at least we shall escape that, even if we do not bring forth Lot to be now as famous a personage as Tut-Ankh-Amen in his modern newspaper

PITCHING TENTS TOWARD SODOM 13

glory. At any rate, we are off from New York for the long voyage, whatever it may have in store for us.

As we drop our pilot near rum-runner's row, I am set to thinking. It has been urged in favour of a great ship subsidy that Americans, the best Americans, practically all Americans going abroad, would surely drop the pilot of American social habits in order to ride on liquor-bearing ships. The outcome does not seem to fulfil that prediction. Our ship, the *America*, is a real "water-wagon," and the company of passengers certainly commends that mode of travel. Here is one of the finest companies of travellers one might ever see; no drinking or carousing, and not a painted face in the whole lot, but people of manifest culture and refinement and elegance in their manner of life.

The United States Lines are doing the utmost that can be done to make the table and service on shipboard such as will attract the travelling public, and seem most likely to succeed in gaining its patronage. They are, indeed, now succeeding, and deserve to succeed completely. They cannot have a ship at every date that may be wanted, so that, of course, it is not to be assumed that every one who travels on a non-prohibition ship does so in order to drink whisky, but ultimately the

American prohibition policy will get the best and the most of the trade.

The tall buildings of New York have aptly been called "modern cliff dwellings." And certainly the windows of dwellers in these flats seem like holes high up in the sides of narrow cañons. The modern ocean liners also seem made on the same model of architecture. The *America* is an eight- or nine-story flat inverted, starting with the roof garden and numbering the flats as one goes down instead of up. We are on the third flat down, with the dining-room on the flat below us. The city pastor who climbs stairs all day long in his pastoral work does not get much change in that respect by an ocean voyage; he feels quite at home mounting the flats of a modern liner.

Sabbath at sea is much what the individual makes it—as it is everywhere else. The ritualists have the advantage of the rest of us, when it comes to arranging a sea service; the uncertainty of a sermon, which may be utilized by some fanatic for propaganda purposes, makes the temptation very great, even to non-ritualists, to read the Episcopal service—and stop.

The selections from the service made by the young rector who presided really gave us a very solemn and impressive half-hour. The helpfulness of it was somewhat lessened, for some of us, however, by the minister's spending Sabbath afternoon playing cards and the evenings of the week taking part in modern dances to jazz music.

But I have said that Sabbath is what the individual makes it; I made it a day of thanksgiving. The uplifting power of thankfulness is one of the vital forces of the universe. How does a bird soar, poising on silent wing on high? No one knows. How does a soul soar? There are many who know that it is on the pinions of thankfulness. I have two or three times in my life set aside a day for personal thanksgiving for things blessedly realized, and have found such lightness thereby as has buoyed me up for long stretches of weary burden-bearing. Optimism may be compared to the airplane that mounts skyward, but thankfulness is a lighter-than-air craft that of itself lifts great weights heavenward, and gives lightness and buoyancy to life for long years afterward. "Let the redeemed of the Lord say so."

Companionships, whether of the sea or of the sea of life, determine the voyage. They are not mere accidents of life, but necessary elements. It is not good for man to be alone. Companionship is the necessary condition of possible betterment. The companionships of a sea voyage are supplied from the passenger list and the library catalogue. The young

Polish gentleman, Mr. ——fsky, stocky, stolid, lumbering in carriage and in thought (in four languages), is an example of what the melting-pot can do when the melting is good. Twenty-nine years of age, twelve years in America, "began to drink, began to gamble, but the grace of God saved me; member of Russian Church then, but Protestant now, and member of Moody Church."

"Are you not afraid to go back so near to Russia?"

"Vell, I said I am going back to see my mother, no matter what happens, for she cry all ze time and say I never come to see *her*."

His explanation of what America had made of him was, "I think it was my mother's prayers." Some notable American workers, Gray and Rader and Philpot, he thought, also had something to do with it. They are showing that foreigners can be Americanized.

But even America needs to be Americanized. Here is a gentleman returning to the Balkans, where he has been engaged in reconstruction work. I said, "You had better keep away from the Balkans." But he replied, "No, it is safer right now in Belgrade, Serbia, than in America. *The most dangerous place in all the civilized world to-day is America.*" Perhaps he is right, since we have more banditry than China, more robbery than the war-torn lands, and more murders than all the rest of the civilized world. There is no greater mission field in the world than the United States of America. Dr. Ferris is with us on her way to the Baroda Mission in India, and we all love to think of America as the "sower that went forth to sow," but we are much in danger of the tragic lamentation, "Mine own vineyard have I not kept."

The companionship of books is as varied as the companionship of persons; a mystery story for mental rest, after-war conditions in Europe for a view of things, a little modern realism only to discover that things are rather smelly, and the *Confessions of a Psychologist* in order to get the invigoration of a cold wave. We used to have the Psychology of Religion, a very helpful discipline; now we have the Religion of Psychology, the refrigeration of all belief, which puts it away in cold storage "for keeps." "Everything comes from within"; all our hopes, all our inspirations, all our revelation, everything natural and supernatural, "All comes from within!" Man makes his own gods; enthrones himself, after dethroning every other.

Verily this is idealism run mad, "Christian Science" in the realm of philosophy; nothing is; we only think so! "Everything comes from within." Will such a religion as this build churches, schools, and hospitals, and sacrifice itself to save a miserable world? Would it even furnish any blessed civilization from which to give out the *Confessions of a Psychologist?*

The Victoria Institute, to attend which I came by way of England, is one of the oldest and most distinguished, and still most conservative, of English institutions. How delightfully and overwhelmingly gratifying to meet with sympathetic friends from among the real scholars of Great Britain—"hands across the sea." They welcomed Americans to help win the Great War and now equally welcome Americans to help win the greater war for the safety of the truth. My friend, Harold M. Wiener, Esq., tells me that the radicals are much disturbed, and well they may be. They have a very pretty theory, of which they are enamoured very much; but facts are final, and the facts are against their theory. Field-men of Bible lands are nearly all facing in the opposite direction from that in which that theory points. Some of these field-men have not, as yet, progressed very far, but it is the direction which determines where one is going.

To be cordially greeted and to hear greetings for the *Sunday School Times,* Xenia Theological Seminary, and *Bibliotheca Sacra,* from the distinguished company that attends the Victoria Institute makes one of the green oases in the desert of research and controversy. It would be well if many American College and Seminary professors should unite with this venerable English scientific society. I counted it a great privilege to be allowed to propose a number of names. I hope the persons proposed will accept election.

The dispassionate discussion in France of after-war conditions and the temperate wording of news dispatches concerning German affairs and conduct is most gratifying. There is a detached attitude in the utterances of the best of the French press that is quite at variance with much that is printed *about* France in America. Manifestly there is going on much work of propagandists—*not* French!

Across Europe by airplane is a dream that has been fulfilled. Regular routes are established from London to Paris, Paris to Berlin, and London to Berlin and Warsaw. We did not journey that way, but came as near to it as can be on land and sea. Plymouth early Monday morning, London Monday evening, Paris Tuesday evening, and the French Riviera Wednesday morning, and now away out past Château D'If, the Prison-Isle of Monte Cristo, and far out upon the Mediterranean Wednesday evening, the good ship *Lotus* bears us onward toward the Pharos, and the Pharaohs, and Bible Lands, to pitch our tents toward Sodom.

LETTER TWO:
LATIN PARISH HOUSE, KERAK, MOAB

The Cities of the Plain have for long centuries inspired fervid imagination—lurid imagination indeed, more lurid than that inspired by anything else short of Dante's Inferno or the Spanish Inquisition. Pilgrims and travellers and soldiers have all alike seen that land under the malign influence of the story of the awful tragedy that befell these doomed cities. So we have been told of "foetid air" and "horrible smells" and "execrable water" and "pestilential desolation" until, it must be confessed, it was with some secret trepidation that we smiled at our friends' fears and set off to go to Sodom and Gomorrah.

Well, we are alive to tell that tale—but not to tell it just yet; it must unfold itself in journalistic fashion, like the Pentateuch, and spring its own surprises upon us. We will pitch our tents, at each camping-ground, and live our life, and say what is to be said there, and then move on, recording each deed and each stay and each move in regular order; and,

PITCHING TENTS TOWARD SODOM 21

when the journey is ended, as it was once before, by the Plains of Moab, the story also will be ended, as was the story of Israel's wanderings. We seemed to lack but one thing, that we did not first climb to the heights of Nebo, to the summit of Pisgah, to get Moses' view of the Promised Land from one extremity to the other, "From Hermon even unto Zoar." Instead we will be content with a look up at the mountain from a motor-boat on the bosom of the Dead Sea.

The starting-point of Lot when he set out to Sodom was at Bethel, the highest northern point in that rocky backbone of the Holy Land which lies parallel to the Jordan Valley. From that vantage-point the selfish eye of Lot perceived the sharp contrast between the barrenness of the central ridge and the fertile greenness of the oasis of the *kikkar;* "the great round," that lay in the appalling depths of the Jordan gorge. Thirty-six years ago I stood for the first time at Bethel, exclaimed over Jerusalem twelve miles away, and peered over the edge of the awful chasm that lies between the Judean ridge and the Wall of Moab on the east at the emerald oasis in the bottom of "the great round" that lured Lot. Now from Jerusalem on the same central high ridge of Palestine we set out to seek the lost Cities of the Plain, Sodom and Gomorrah.

The Land of Moab is an old land, but the Trans-Jordania government is a very new government, trying to establish itself in the ways of civilized nations, and it had just occurred to the authorities that one of the ways of civilized peoples is to charge for a look—a visa is the diplomatic word which sounds better, but costs the same! So we were summoned to a dingy office of a Jerusalem business man who had been designated as Consular Agent for the Trans-Jordania government. We learned to our surprise that our visas were to be absolutely the very first granted to anybody by the new government. Moab had enjoyed an evil reputation for some thousands of years, and we could not escape from some disturbing imaginings of thieving parties who might strip us naked and send us back thus to civilization, or of some blood-thirsty cut-throats who would feed our bodies to the buzzards.

Mention of a journey to such a land starts visions of camel trains and Bedouin tents, of flowing robes and white turbans and everything that is usually supposed to make up a patriarchal retinue. If the truth must be told, it was "Uncle Henry"—personifying our Ford motor cars—who took us a hundred miles through eastern Moab to old Kerak.

Careful domestic arrangements must also

be made for such a journey as we were undertaking, for the hotel accommodations at Sodom to-day are not, to say the least, very luxurious, whatever they may have been in the days of Lot. So we had to take along a cook, pots and pans to cook things in, victuals to put in the pots and pans and liquid fuel to make a fire underneath. Canned fruits and vegetables and preserves we carried along from Jerusalem, rice and salt and flour we bought later in Kerak, and had bread baked by Bedouin women in their villages down on the Plain, or by the muleteers in the ashes of their campfire. It was alarmingly dirty, but sufficiently well-cooked to make it safe; besides, we took treatment with typhoid serum before starting!

It was a most beautiful morning, February the fourteenth, on which we loaded our four Ford cars even to the mud-guards, said good-bye to loved ones as cheerfully as we could, and dashed off down the Jericho road on the way to the Land of Moab. A letter from a far-off friend the evening before had brought a story of answered prayer not surpassed since the days of Peter and Cornelius, and a sweet peace of faith so filled the soul as to banish all the lurid imaginings concerning the mysterious land to which we journeyed.

The Jericho road is too much a part of civilization, since the war times turned it into one of the finest highways of the world, to enter into an account of a journey to such an out-of-the-world place as the Cities of the Plain. So while we rush down, down, down, by the Apostles' Spring and the Good Samaritan Inn and the Brook Cherith, I will introduce the members of the staff organized for this expedition of Xenia Theological Seminary, in coöperation with the American School of Oriental Research at Jerusalem, that it may appear clearly that there was nothing sectarian in the expedition and that the strictly scientific character of the work may be assured. This, to the end that the results of the expedition may meet with acceptance in every part of the Biblical world.

The President of the staff was the President of Xenia Theological Seminary, Saint Louis, Missouri, U. S. A., who happens to be a United Presbyterian. The director of field operations was Director Albright of the American School of Oriental Research at Jerusalem. Dr. Albright is a Methodist, the son of a South American missionary near Santiago, Chile. He received his university training at Johns Hopkins. He was appointed to his position, one of the most important in the archaeological world, because of his unusual qualifications as an archaeologist and philologist. Our geologist was Professor Alfred Day of Beirut Col-

PITCHING TENTS TOWARD SODOM 25

lege, Syria, a man of long years' experience in the land and thoroughly familiar with the geology of the particular region to which we were going, having made two or three previous expeditions into the same region for geological work.

The proto-archaeologist of the staff, the flint and old stone expert, was Père Mallon, a Jesuit priest, of Ratisbon, Jerusalem. He is a well-known specialist in this field of research with many years of experience in Bible lands. He aided also materially in furnishing out the expedition and in securing us accommodations at the Parish House in Kerak, whence this letter is written. Na'im Makhouli, a representative of the Department of Antiquities of the Palestinian government, gave a semi-official character to our expedition and by his technical knowledge and his perfect acquaintance with the vernacular rendered invaluable assistance. Mr. Makhouli is a member of the Greek Catholic Church in Palestine.

Two Fellows assisted also in the work; William Carroll, the Thayer Fellow of the American School, was a graduate of Yale Divinity School and a member of the Church of God in Ohio. Herbert H. Tay, a Fellow of Xenia Theological Seminary, belongs to the Brethren of California. Two students accompanied us, Mr. Homer B. Kent of Xenia Theological Seminary, also of the Brethren of California, and Mr. E. L. Sukenik, a Russian Jew educated at Berlin. He was our surveyor and field botanist. We had in addition the advice of Mr. Dinsmore of Jerusalem, of the American Colony, the most expert botanist in Palestine. Upon our return, we submitted our evidence to the judgment of Père Vincent, the foremost Palestinian scholar in the world, and professor in L'Ecole Saint Etienne, Jerusalem, and also to Phythian-Adams of the Palestine Exploration Society who was just being ordained to the priesthood in the Anglican Church.

This unusual combination of faiths certainly relieves the expedition of any possible suspicion of sectarianism. All these were men of devout reverence for the Old Testament Scriptures, which represents the field of our operations. It is a pleasure to say that we worked together in the greatest harmony, and our conclusions were, I think without exception, unanimous.

An account of the journey around through eastern Moab to Kerak and from there down to the Plain at the Lisan near the lower end of the Dead Sea, if it approached to the interest of the journey itself, would be very entertaining, but a statement of the results of the expedition will require so much time that the

PITCHING TENTS TOWARD SODOM 27

incidents of the journey must be passed over with scant notice. We went down by the great military road from Jerusalem to Jericho, crossed the river on the Allenby bridge and went on by way of Es Salt and Amman, the capital of Trans-Jordania, to Kerak, the ancient Kir of Moab, the base from which we were to carry on our work.

All the diplomatic machinery was new, and worked slowly. At the Allenby bridge over the Jordan we met the passport officers. They looked at our passports and examined those visas, front and back and right side up and wrong side up, and then all over again, to be sure that they were doing things right, but finally decided that all was regular; and we paid our toll for the autos, and entered the Land of Moab. It is most interesting to see the beginnings of a nation's efforts to rise and take its place in the family. These people mean well, and they are trying very hard to win esteem, and are deserving of it; but, oh, they are so poor!

We followed the old Roman road, now partly re-made, to Es Salt and Amman. It is a most picturesque way up the gorge from the Jordan valley to the highlands. At times it wound in and out of the sinuosities of the mountain-side with a precipice above us and another below, and with one hair-pin curve after another. We kept on it when we had to and kept off it when we could, for it was very rough. At Es Salt, in the Land of Gilead, in the old territory of Gad, is a mountain city of fifteen thousand people in a fine agricultural country. It is a turbulent place, in which there had been a bloody riot but a short time before.

After cooling our engines from the heat of the steep climb, we soon ran out upon the beautiful upland plains of Amman. As I looked far over the well-cultivated fields, I understood why Reuben, Gad, and Manasseh wished to remain on this side Jordan rather than to pass over to the stony hills of the Promised Land.

But where are the people? Surely they do not live in the city, miles away from these farm lands. Yet hour after hour we run on without meeting a person or seeing any one in the fields, or even discovering a village. In this is vividly portrayed the fear in which for centuries the people have lived, so marked that they have learned to hide their dwellings in some deep wady and keep themselves out of sight. But an auto breaks down, and in a few minutes two men are seen hastening toward us, one of them carrying a gun; presently three more appear with another gun, and in a short time women and children join the

PITCHING TENTS TOWARD SODOM 29

company, until there are twenty to thirty gathered.

To rob us? Not at all; simply to gratify curiosity. The gun-carrying is a habit of worse days than the present. One seems never alone in this land, however invisible the population may be. Stop, and in a few minutes people seem to rise out of the ground.

Early in the evening we came down into the beautiful valley of the City of Waters, the Rabbath Amman of the days of the Kingdom of Israel, where for long was kept the bed of Og, King of Bashan (Deut. 3:11). I climbed to the great Acra that crowns the high hill north of the valley, and stumbled over the almost cyclopean ruins of Roman days, against one of the fiercest and most fitful winds I ever faced. If one looked into a great cistern, one moment he was in danger of being pushed in by the sheer force of the wind, and the next in danger of losing his balance and pitching in, when the wind suddenly ceased!

In vain I tried to conjure up the picture of the glory of Roman days, when the palaces of the rich lined the sides of this deep vale, and yonder great Roman theatre with its ten thousand seats resounded with the clamour of the exulting multitude gloating over the gladiatorial shows and the onslaughts of wild beasts; but imagination faltered on the wing, and I came down to drink the sweet, pure water from the fountain and enjoy the novelty of tenting in the open square in front of the Emir's palace.

Our tent life involved some roughing it, but no real hardship. We had good double tents, comfortable cots, warm wraps, abundance of good food well-cooked and served; and each one helped with the work of the tents. We were a company of Bible students; we read and discussed the Biblical record; said grace at our meals, had morning prayers together and our evening devotions individually, and planned a service for each Sabbath. With a few exceptions under peculiar circumstances, these plans were carried out, and there was a blessed sense of a common faith and a common share in a gracious providence that constantly opened the way and smoothed out our difficulties and ministered to our comfort and safety.

At Amman we had to tarry a little, to complete our diplomatic arrangements with the government for permission and protection. We had a friend at court, Riza Tewfik Pasha, head of the Department of Antiquities of Trans-Jordania, a genial, cultivated Turkish gentleman who introduced us to the Prime Minister. Within one hour—not a year, or a month, or a week, as in the old Turkish days, but an hour—there was put into our hands a letter to the Governor of Kerak empowering him to furnish us an escort and to further our expedition.

The Sabbath day was to be a day of rest, but the first Sabbath saw a disturbance of our plans, and we were forced to make a "sabbath day's journey." Saturday night the wind blew from the west, and the west wind brings rain, and the rain came, and, as the wind blew, it grew colder, and the clouds most ominously promised snow. Camping out in the snow in February on the highlands of Amman was not to be risked. It was unanimously decided that we must seek shelter. The tents were struck, and the autos loaded, and we rushed on over —not the Roman road any more—but a desert trail around the head waters of the Arnon and through eastern Moab to the old fortress city of Kerak—Kir of Moab of the days of the Conquest, perched on its mountain summit more than three thousand feet above sea level.

Once and again and again our dilapidated cars—derelicts left, by the way, from the Great War—broke down. The last time caused so long a delay, while the would-be mechanics, our Arab chauffeurs, tried to make repairs, that darkness overtook us before we reached our destination. Night is the time of mystery and of danger in this land; but, being caught out on the road, we could do nothing but keep on our way however great the alarm and anxiety.

Amusing incidents will obtrude in the most tragic situations. Some of our company, unused to Oriental wiles, had been talking rather freely in English under the impression that they were not understood. From my seat by the chauffeur, from whom I could get nothing but Arabic grunts, I had uttered a warning that Arabs were not always as ignorant as they looked. As we rounded the corner of the mountain and lights appeared in the distance, I summoned what little possibility there seemed of conversation with my seat-mate and, pointing to the lights, said, "Kerak?" The response was the rapid fire of English which I had suspected all the time was under his tarboush!

How good the lights of that Moabite city looked as we wound along the precipitous sides of the *wady*, and climbed the last steep hill, and reported our arrival to the governor. Arrangements had been made with the Christian and Missionary Alliance at Jerusalem that one of their missionaries located at Kerak should make arrangements for our entertainment at some house in the town. But when we had reported our arrival at the Governorate, a native Christian helper came to us

PITCHING TENTS TOWARD SODOM 33

from the mission house to say that the missionary was very sick and could not meet us, but that if we would come to his home he would help us with advice so far as he could.

We sent our thanks and our sympathy, but declined to trouble a sick man at nine o'clock at night with a lot of fine husky archaeologists. Père Mallon said, "I will go and see what I can do at the parish house." He soon returned with the Arabic answer, "Peace." In colloquial English, "It is all right."

At the Latin parish house the priest, a gentle invalid, received us most kindly, put the large salon at our disposal for our cots, and gave us a kitchen and a dining-room, and good water. We soon had a hot dinner, and had made our beds, and then we gathered for the service we had arranged for the morning when the threatening snowstorm had scattered us. The Word was read, with heartfelt comments upon God's goodness to us in giving safety and shelter in abundance, and then one after another offered prayer and thanksgiving.

Warmed and fed and blessed with a sense of His nearness, we lay down and slept in "peace." A predatory cat had hid, like Saul of old, among the stuff, and in the night could not resist the temptation to respond to the challenge of his enemy on the wall outside. I heard nothing of the duel. "You certainly sleep the sleep of the just," was the comment of Dr. Albright. For me it was truly "peace."

LETTER THREE:
AT CAMP IN HENZIREH, MOAB

I am in a most perplexing uncertainty concerning the place at which I left off transcribing my notes in my last letter. Indeed, one out here seems to have gotten into another state of existence, where the ordinary laws of sequence do not hold and where the former world in which we lived has been left so far behind that even the ordinary habits of thought have lost their potency or—run off the track. In this land of primitive things we seem to have been suddenly transported into the patriarchal world, and it seems as if it were a former age and another state of existence, in which we actually moved in civilization. Well, anyway, if I omit something, you will not miss it, and if I repeat something, just charge it to the ineffectual effort I am making to adapt myself to such strange circumstances.

If this introduction fails to introduce anything, it will have served exactly the purpose for which it is intended, to show the utter break with all our civilized Occidental life which one undergoes in coming to the Land of Moab.

PITCHING TENTS TOWARD SODOM 35

Ordinary folks who come to America are not expected to call upon the President or even his Secretary of State, but very distinguished guests give attention to such formalities. In the Land of Moab, almost any foreigner is a distinguished guest, and especially a company of Americans come to study Biblical sites. So our first act, the morning after arrival at the old fortress city of Kerak, or Kir of Moab, must be to make formal call upon the Governor of Kerak.

Rachid Pasha is rather a handsome man who has surrounded himself with a tawdry Oriental pomp and with military discipline, and is withal, like so many Orientals, a polyglot man, who accommodated his guests by talking now Arabic, now French and now, for the benefit of some of us, even a little English. He saluted, and we saluted, as each one entered. Then, after introductions, he bade us be seated, and sat down himself. Then he immediately saluted again, and we responded.

From time to time a servant entered, saluted, advanced and presented some papers or delivered a verbal message, and then retired backward to the door. State duties did not seem to press, or Oriental courtesy required that they should wait, for a desultory conversation dragged along for about three-quarters of an hour before coffee was served. The longer that rite is delayed, the greater the honour that is showed the guests.

All this was not empty form, for he was most kindly in all his dealings with us, and at this interview introduced us to the Sheik of the district to which we were going, who, having drunk coffee with us—all out of one cup—was pledged by laws of hospitality for our safety and comfort. A military escort was at once provided, and a letter given us to the commander of the garrison on the Plain, directing that his fifty soldiers should guard us from every danger and annoyance. These people are determined to show the Western world that they can be civilized and govern themselves. President Wilson's ideal of self-determination has taken deep root and is sending up vigorous governmental shoots in strange and unexpected places.

Even archaeologists must give first place to the living present, so that, after our visit of respect to the Governor, we pay another to the American missionary and his wife and little child. This isolated family ministers in this patriarchal graveyard, seemingly dead since the days of Abraham (yet what anomalies are here, for Professor Day bought a battery for his flashlight in Kerak!). The romance of missions is certainly not all gone, driven into exile by the infiltration of civiliza-

PITCHING TENTS TOWARD SODOM 37

tion's novelties. Here is a delightful, cultivated family living in a rough stone Kerak house among the fanatical people of this forgotten land, and preaching the Evangel and living its message of good-will to men.

I said to Dr. Albright, "These frontier missionaries are the self-sacrificing ones of earth."

"Don't I know?" said he. "I am a child of a missionary home." Even the priest at the parish house at which we stopped told a pathetic tale of loneliness in his ministering to several little flocks, totalling only about one hundred souls. A sombreness colours everything here, from the days of Israel's invasion down to the fanatical rule of Moslems of to-day.

Kir of Moab figures largely in the early history of Bible lands. Here it was, most probably, that Ehud, the second of the Judges, slew Eglon, king of Moab, and freed Israel from Moabite domination. Here Jehoram, allied with Jehoshaphat, pressed the siege so hard that the king of Moab took the crown prince and offered him as a burnt offering on the wall. Upon these great walls that now engirdle the city? No, these walls, which the Turks breached to keep the people of Kerak from revolting, were built by the Crusaders and the Arabs.

38 EXPLORATIONS AT SODOM

Round about these walls we go, seeking evidence of an earlier Kir, the Kir of ancient Israel, and find not a trace. Where was the ancient Kir? Now that preliminary courtesies were over, work must begin; having paid our respects to the living, we turn to the business of the expedition, the investigation of the dead.

The early morning was rather impossible for archaeological research, for we are more than three thousand feet above sea level, five thousand feet above the Dead Sea, and also were above the clouds, or in the midst of them. It reminded me of Chikungshan in China, where I went up into the clouds, stayed up in the clouds, preached in the clouds, and came down out of the clouds—and did not see the place at all. But by the time our visits were finished, the clouds were lifting and we set out to explore.

We made most careful search for the site of the old Kir of Moab, but, for a time, quite unsuccessfully. We walked about this old impregnable fortress, climbed up to the top of its Crusader towers, peered into its many tunnels, dark, crooked, and difficult, and looked down from its dizzy heights. We photographed some of its old Greek gravestones, which proved to be Christian, of the seventh or eighth century. We even ventured into the precincts of the barracks, and were challenged

PITCHING TENTS TOWARD SODOM 39

by the guard, but later were admitted by the commanding officer.

Yet all this was to no good result in our search. There were plenty of Arabic ruins, with here and there some relics from Byzantine times, and overtopping everything else there were the marks of the Crusader, but no sign of ancient Kir. Our purpose is to get scientific evidence of the city of the days of the Israelite invasion, something to establish impregnably the historical sanctions of the Biblical references to Moab, if such be here.

Our search on the top of the hill where the city ought to have been had yielded us nothing. At noon around the table we had better news. Professor Day, who had been spying about the foundations of the hill on which the city was built—"geologizing," as he called his investigations—had found the old pottery of the later Bronze Age in that land. Here certainly was the evidence we sought, but where was Kir?

We were disposed to jeer, and said, "Nobody ever built a city on the slope of precipice."

Then Dr. Albright said, "I will tell you what it means; the buildings now above that precipice are Crusader works. The Crusaders were Europeans who cleared the ground before they built, instead of building on top of the tell, as the Orientals did. So they shoved the rubbish of the old Kir right over the edge of the precipice, and there Professor Day found it."

Now the whole case was clear enough. This rubbish heap is not where the ancient city was, but where the rubbish of that city was emptied over the cliff. There, above the heap, frown the walls of the Crusaders. Being wont to sweep the ground on which they built, they threw the sweepings, in this case, down this east hill, and here they lie to tell the tale. Up there, then, on the summit, had been Kir of Moab.

To confirm this conclusion two things were needed, the spring, or other convenient water supply, and the High Place for worship. The first of these appeared instantly, for from the very place at which we stood there led a well-made pathway along the rocky ledge of the mountain side to a spring of excellent water in the valley to the southeast. It was rather suggestive to find the water somewhat sulphurous! Were we not going to seek Sodom, and even now drawing nigh?

Along this rocky path a cave was found, and from the cave a well-cut tunnel led into the mountain. A venturesome guide who rushed along in the dark fell into a pit twelve feet deep. After he was hauled out, another pit a little way on was found over which it

RUINS OF FORTRESS
ERECTED TO PROTECT
THE GREAT HIGH PLACE

did not seem safe to venture. The burning of some calcium wire showed the direction of the tunnel. It led directly toward the castle on the hill, a secret passageway toward the spring when enemies lurked around, affording a means of securing water without forsaking cover. Subsequent examination found the end of the tunnel at about six hundred feet. For some reason unknown to us, it was abandoned.

One last needed touch of evidence concerning the old-time heathen city was still wanting. Now we knew the spring at which these ancient people of Kir quenched their thirst—where did they seek to refresh their souls? Where was the High Place, and what was it like? It was hardly to be expected that we would find that, as it might have been among the débris swept away by the Crusaders. Here we were happily disappointed, however, or at least surprised. Mr. Carroll, Thayer Fellow of the American School at Jerusalem, came in one afternoon from a ramble over the surrounding mountains with a report of a High Place on the top of the highest mountain, surmounting even the summit on which the old city stood.

Early next morning, while the muleteers packed up their loads for our journey down to the Plain of Sodom and Gomorrah, he led some of us to see that grim but silent messenger from the ancient heathen world. It was a long, hard early morning walk, but it well repaid the effort. South of the height on which old Kir stood and separated from that height by a narrow gorge, afterwards turned into a moat by the Crusaders, we climbed to an overtopping height, up, up, up, until all the world around seemed beneath us. There, on a great flat rock, the uncut natural altar was found.

It was not a fabricated altar. The early Canaanites seldom, if ever, had such. There were no standing stones, but only the flat natural rock of the mountain, with quite a series of the mysterious cup-marks which are ofttimes a puzzle to every archaeologist. They probably had different uses under different circumstances. But these were certainly somehow connected with the devotions of the people. Cup-marks are sometimes found in connection with oil presses, but not so here, for the big cup-marks on this rock drained into the little ones. Here on this mountain-top, the people of ancient Kir gathered, far from the distractions of business or pleasure or labour, and performed—what strange, perhaps horrid rites? Some prince, as in the days of Jehoshaphat, may have been immolated on this rock, and libations been poured in these cup-marks to some bloodthirsty god.

But where, we asked, was the pathway to

PITCHING TENTS TOWARD SODOM 43

this altar? Immediately our eyes answered our own question. For there, a little to one side of the way we had approached, was a well-marked and well-graded path leading directly from the place of the Citadel, below, to the High Place.

On the way down, as we hurried back—for the call to be on the way down to the Plain was strong upon us—we most unexpectedly came upon another High Place, with equal certainty a primitive High Place, with only the flat rock and its cup-marks. This was down quite near the city itself. The great High Place was manifestly on the mountain-top far withdrawn from the bustle of business and pleasure, while here, near at hand, was a shrine to which the busy and hurried could come and pour a libation to some frightful heathen deity—and lose no more time than a modern worshipper who tells his beads!

Here, then, was Kir of Moab about the time of the Conquest of Israel; here its citadel, and yonder its spring, and this its place of worship. The claims of the Bible for this region at that period are quite substantiated. The mention of Moab at that period of the world's history was no anachronism; nor, for that matter, was the inscription of Rameses the Great, which I found in 1908, on the base of the statue at the temple of Luxor, in which

44   EXPLORATIONS AT SODOM

he boasts of having conquered Moab (*Recueil de Traveaix*, 27, p. 18). Items of evidence seem to come from the ends of the earth to meet and certify the claims of the old Book. Is it any wonder that some who know these facts become so confident in their belief in the integrity of the Bible that they scarce take time to look at new pieces of evidence, but in calm assurance say, with the Psalmist, "I have stuck unto the testimonies"?

Supplied with our letter from the genial governor, Rachid Pasha, to the garrison on the Plain, and given, for a consideration, an escort of soldiers, we mounted, and rode away from Kir of Moab.

LETTER FOUR:
CAMP WADY, NUMEIRAH

I have been to dinner, "not where one eats, but where one is eaten." I had gone outside my tent to sit in the evening twilight after supper. I rested on a great block of red sandstone. Presently I felt a pinch on the back of my hand, and grabbed at a little hard dark object which I could not clearly see. Then there was another and another pinch, until I discovered that I had my feet in a great ant-hill of big black ants. They had crawled up my trouser-legs; presently they made them-

PITCHING TENTS TOWARD SODOM 45

selves felt all over me, and I had to strip to the skin, turn my garments inside out and shake them.

Before supper I had had a bath, a real bath in the most wonderful bathroom. The base was cretaceous limestone, the side walls old red sandstone, and the ceiling blue sky, in which the stars presently shone. The bathtub was made of boulders round about and had a sanded bottom; and I bathed in running water as pure and clear as crystal, the waters of Wady Numeirah. Before my bath I had gone up the wady to the spring, amidst tropical foliage where the water comes down over the precipice of red sandstone.

Such were experiences of our camp at Wady Numeirah as we came down from the Mountains of Moab, down, down, down, five thousand feet to the Plain at Ghor-Es-Safieh, twelve hundred feet below sea level. Our camp, from which we set out in the morning, was above a copious fountain by a sombre stone village, mud-plastered, on the highland of Moab. The village rejoiced in the plebeian name of Henzireh, the Sow. There are said to be about one hundred houses and nine hundred inhabitants. Apparently the houses are "apartment houses," with a rather smaller allotment of space to the individual than even in some American apartments.

The ride over the rough mountain trail was rather uninteresting in itself, but the views were sometimes wonderful and most enticing. Here and there, as we looked down a wady that led toward the sea, a marvellous vista of Palestine across the sea opened up. As the sun shone out fitfully it lighted up now one spot, now another, in the hills of Judaea.

The illuminated places seemed to our eyes like glimpses of heaven. How like this must have been the experience of the Children of Israel as they passed up north along this way, and now and again caught glimpses of the Promised Land!

Had we known what was before us in the day's journey we might not have been able to enjoy these quiet visions. The descent into the Grand Canyon of Arizona is held out as one of the sensational allurements of venturesome travel in America, and it is indeed sufficiently terrifying to frighten many people against undertaking it. But the descent into the Grand Canyon is but a delightful holiday experience, compared with the descent from the Mountains of Moab to Wady Numeirah. We dismounted, but found it a difficult task even to walk down that treacherous trail. We walked, when we could, and climbed when we could not walk, and slid when we could not climb.

PITCHING TENTS TOWARD SODOM 47

I saw a mule, trained to his goat-like task on mountain trails, stiffen his fore-legs on the sloping surface of a rock and slide down until his feet found a resting-place. The cliff was almost perpendicular, and the trail thus necessarily a constant zigzag. It was tacking on the mountain side, and oftentimes there was a new tack every rod of progress. The trail was filled with great stones, between which our feet sank into dust and sand, and at best there was but a narrow path, sometimes only a foot or two in width. If one slipped over the edge he might lodge anywhere, within a thousand feet!

One muleteer allowed his mule to pick his own way, and, as is the way with mulishness, the animal perversely walked out of the path on the edge of the precipice. Some men are like that mule, they will not keep in the beaten pathways of life. Business men often venture into devious economic by-paths; some preachers even are known to have an itch for making people jumpy by their startling theological vagaries, and politicians are always on the jagged edge of things. This mule became a warning to all such mules and men as will not keep in the beaten path. We recovered his load, which happened to include my bed, but the mule himself did not recover!

Some of us, unencumbered, walked on ahead

to the place of camp at the foot of the precipice. Then for hours we watched the pack-train slowly working its way down. It was nine at night before the last load was safely deposited at the green tents. The bringing of those last loads was the occasion of an interesting scene and a striking illustration. Some loads had been left on the mountain, because the animals were too heavily loaded to make the descent, and some men and mules had to return for a second descent of part of the way. No one was willing to go.

As a matter of course, a row soon brewed, until at last the soldiers interfered and compelled some of the muleteers to go. Several personal encounters occurred in this strife, and, when they came to blows, a third man would always rush in and lay a hand upon each one in the quarrel; when they always separated and allowed him to compose their differences. Here was the "daysman," the "mediator" making peace! It was worth that hard and perilous afternoon to observe this sight. Only when these Oriental customs embodied in Old Testament lore and in the theology of the Bible are actually seen does all the Scripture vividness become apparent.

A bounteous and appetizing hot dinner, such as our cook was wont to serve up to us, and such a night of rest as mountain climbing and

PITCHING TENTS TOWARD SODOM 49

mountain air induce, sent us down the wady next morning in the best of spirits. The trail was in the very bottom of the wady and rather easy going. The vivid colours of the rocks ranged from the white and yellow of the limestone base to the gorgeous hues of the old red sandstone that towered above. About ten o'clock we got our first good view of the Sea and the Plain, and began the last stage of the descent, some twelve hundred feet of the yellow cliffs at the bottom.

After an hour of rapid going we came out of the wady almost on the level, and found ourselves on the top of the last mountain peak, twelve hundred feet high. It seemed so to us, yet according to the customary way of measuring levels that was not a mountain-top at all, but a hole in the ground; for this mountain-top was actually some fifty feet below sea-level. It gave us a queer feeling to realize that we were already below sea-level, but had yet twelve hundred feet more to descend before we reached the edge of the lowest sheet of water in the world, and could pitch our camp in the lowest oasis on the surface of the earth.

We lunched in the saddle. One soon marvels at the unnecessary refinements of civilization on such a journey as this. I quickly learned to lunch on horseback. With a loaf of Arab bread folded and thrust into one overcoat pocket, a big piece of chocolate in another pocket, and two hard-boiled eggs in still another with my Baedeker, "the table was set." I found it was quite possible to get the shells off the eggs, and to eat them with alternate bites of bread and chocolate, without losing hold of the halter-rope of my pony or letting an egg fall—or swallowing the shells.

We scrambled and slid down these last slopes, and dipped our hands in the oily waters of the Dead Sea, stumbled over the driftwood that lines the shore, and then mounted our horses and rode on in the noonday heat, the most tropical we had yet experienced.

LETTER FIVE:
CAMP AT GHOR-ES-SAFIEH, MOAB

A great surprise awaited us at our camping place. The travellers who have been here, from the pilgrims of the Middle Ages to the Biblical students of modern time, and even some scientists who have been here recently and have written descriptions of the Plain, have given us lurid, and even gruesome, descriptions of this region. Our first shock was to come to a great water-course much wider than the channel of the Jordan, and so filled with boulders distributed by the water as to tell of

PITCHING TENTS TOWARD SODOM 51

terrific floods of water at times. Rushing along this course was a stream, twenty feet wide and nearly a foot deep, of the clearest and purest water from that great red sandstone range above us. I have never drunk better spring water anywhere in the world.

Presently we came upon one and another and another little zigzag canal, irrigating ditches, drawing off this water for the fields of the Bedouin. And there the fields were, delighting the eye, lush fields of timothy and clover, reminding me of my farmer-boy days, and luxuriant fields of wheat almost ready to head out; while here and there were most thrifty fig orchards and vineyards, the vines sometimes on the ground, sometimes trained up systematically on an excellent trellis. Great fields of dura uncultivated, and still other fields of dura stalks from last year's crops, are seen. The indigo plant, also, is cultivated.

Something like ten thousand acres could be watered from this one stream. We never suffered from the heat by day, and at night the temperature fell to about sixty-five degrees. The air was dry, pure, and bracing, and the reputed "horrid smells" and "pestilential swamps" can hardly be said to exist. How could it be so where the intensity of the saltness of the water tends to purify everything it touches?

52 EXPLORATIONS AT SODOM

Those who have written of this place have done so under the spell of the dreadful tragedy which took place here. They have not been untruthful, but psychology sometimes makes people "see things." The truth is that, when Palestine becomes prosperous—and she is rapidly becoming so—an automobile line from Jerusalem to the Dead Sea and a motor-boat line on the sea will make this one of the finest winter health resorts in the world. It has far more romantic beauty and grandeur of scenery than Luxor, with almost none of the annoyances of that Egyptian resort. A Californian in our party said the climate was "just like home," and with a Californian there is nothing beyond that—except heaven. In truth, the only correct description ever written of the material conditions of life in this place of which I have any knowledge is that in the book of Genesis, "Like the garden of the Lord."

If we are finding mistakes in travellers' accounts of this place, it is not so with the Biblical account. God rained fire and brimstone upon the Cities of the Plain. Now, brimstone is brimstone, even though used in a miracle. And a region on which brimstone was rained will show brimstone. Well, it does; we picked up pure sulphur, in pieces as big as the end of my thumb. It is mixed with the marl of the mountains on the west side of the sea, and now is to be found scattered along the shore of the sea even on the east side, some four or five miles distant from the ledge that contains the stratum. It has been somehow *scattered* far and wide over this Plain. Indeed, sulphur seems to be rather widely distributed in this part of the world, when we recall the sulphur in the water of the spring at Kerak.

Some people are quite distracted trying to harmonize science and the Bible. It is wasted effort. Science, when it is true knowledge of the facts of nature, cannot be otherwise than harmonious with any other true statement of facts, as we constantly find the Bible to be. *Truth is harmonious everywhere.* Our frantic efforts to make harmonize things that do not seem to do so, usually result in our paring down some truth, or rounding off its corners, to make it fit some of our preconceived and mistaken notions. We need only to find truth; when found it will be found to be harmonious with all other truth.

Our safety down on the Plain was a constant source of satisfaction and thanksgiving. Our soldiers were most watchful, to warn us of any approach to wild Arabs, of which there are still some in Moab. And when we stopped to pitch our green tents beside one of the swift little canals of sweet water, there, beside the next one, were the white tents, like Indian tepees, of the garrison of fifty soldiers encamped here. We called upon the colonel, and he called upon us, and, as long as we stayed, the soldiers stayed beside us day and night.

We reached this camping-place about the end of the week, and it was with peculiar feelings of gratitude to God that we awoke on the Sabbath to rest and to worship. The cook said ten o'clock would suit best for service, our service for the staff in English. Père Mallon held a service at seven o'clock for the Christian Arabs, of whom we had seven. Then, promptly at ten, we all gathered for worship.

Preaching at Sodom was a novel and dramatic experience. Our Lord said that, if such things as were done at Capernaum had been done at Sodom, the cities would have continued. They were not done then. It would not do to say the Gospel has never been preached at Sodom, for in Byzantine times there was a bishop in the region and probably a church at Zoar, but in modern times—well, I wonder if ever before in later centuries a sermon has been preached here.

It seemed a unique privilege as I preached that morning on the Joy of Triumph, the Triumph of Faith, from Paul's exultant cry at the prospect of the crown, when he had finished

PITCHING TENTS TOWARD SODOM 55

his course. So blessed had been the providential arrangements for our work, and so prosperous all our journey to this place, that now, as we were ready to begin our researches, we were able in faith to look forward to success and to enter into the spirit of Paul's words of triumph.

Many travellers have been to the region of the Cities of the Plain, from the Palestine pilgrims onward. Some of these, as De Saulcy, and Lynch, Robinson and Tristram and Hull, have written most entertainingly. Some scientists also have been here, and have given the world valuable information: Lynch, the geographer and hydrographer, whose work is standard to this day; Wright and Blankenkorn, geologists who settled most geological questions concerning this region; and Huntington, who, despite his absurdities concerning the location of Sodom and the level of the Dead Sea in the days of Abraham, yet wrote helpfully concerning the transformation of Palestine. Also, the surveyors of the Archaeological Survey of Palestine planned this region, and put it on their maps.

Yet in truth no real archaeological survey of this region had ever been made. Palestinian Archaeology as a science is quite new. It is but recently that knowledge concerning the various ages of civilization in that land have accumulated sufficiently to allow a proper systematization and classification, and only after such classification is it possible to make a real scientific survey of any particular part of the land.

Now, some objector will interpose the impatient question, "Why is it that you archaeologists, whenever you talk about ancient civilization, begin to prattle about potsherds? Would not artifacts of bronze or iron or wood, or some textile fabrics, be a far better evidence concerning civilization?"

Why, of course they would—if we had them. But those things have nearly all perished. The wood has rotted; the cloth has been destroyed by moth and mildew; iron has left little but a spot of rust; and even the bronze is ofttimes much eaten away by chemicals in the soil. But pottery, being of clay and burned, abides and thus is often about the only evidence of civilization left to us.

Without claiming absolute accuracy for the science of pots, even admitting that some take their accuracy in reading the lore of pottery too seriously, yet it is possible to apply most satisfactory general tests that determine with reasonable accuracy and, within quite narrow limits, the character and age of a Palestinian civilization, from the potsherds found in the débris which that age has left. Thus, if a civilization which the Bible represents to have existed in a certain place at a certain time be examined, the potsherds will tell the same story concerning the character and age of that civilization as the Bible, and where the silence of the Bible denotes the absence of a civilization, the potsherds will tell the same tale.

In a word, here is the criterion for all our researches at the Cities of the Plain. The story of Abraham and of Sodom and Gomorrah in Genesis represents a Canaanite civilization on this Plain in the twentieth century B.C., the Early Bronze Age in Palestinian history. This civilization, the Bible tells us, was destroyed by a fearful catastrophe that blasted the region, and from that time on in Biblical history a most significant silence envelops this whole region. Even Jehoshaphat, when he attacked the King of Moab, went around it. The Bible knows nothing more, historically, of a civilization here.

Now, an archaeological survey will find the same story in potsherds, if the historical sanctions of the Biblical history are really secured. If they are not secured, it will ever remain for sceptical criticism to put an interrogation point after the story of the Cities of the Plain. To find this story in the potsherds was what had never been done, and in this our task was clearly marked out.

We set ourselves the task of combing this whole Plain, to see if it yielded these historical sanctions of the Biblical story. Thus only, if we can certify the Sodom civilization, is it worth while to seek for the Sodom location. But when we locate the civilization, it will be located *somewhere,* and we shall seek to determine the exact place.

Life is a continual discovery, the joy of living is the joy of that unfolding of life which makes up its discoveries, and each new day is such a field of discovery upon which we have alighted. So our work of discovery on the Plain will give most joy to the reader if it be allowed to unfold day by day, as we found it.

Report of some things had come to us before we reached the Plain, and we naturally turned to examine these things first. There was Lubrous, more properly El Ubrous, which General Kitchener thought to be the ruins of ancient Zoar. Its commanding height stood out at the side of the Plain, and towards its ruins we turned our steps—rather, our horses' steps. The search led us up the course of the river toward the mountains of Moab on the east, and then up the heights to the long, low grey ridge which fronts the red sandstone mountains of Moab, which glare down upon the sea.

PITCHING TENTS TOWARD SODOM 59

Here we found remains of immense stone structures, with cyclopean stones in the walls fronting the Plain—but the work was Crusader, some perhaps Arabic, and a little Byzantine. There was not a trace of the early Palestinian civilization here. Indeed, high above this fortress, on the top of the long narrow range, was a watch tower, and a little below on a kind of wide flat ledge of the mountain was a stone corral for horses—the Crusaders' horses?

But the archaeologist finds not a trace of any city of homes or of the daily home-life of a people here in this waterless place. On the other hand, down there along the deep wady below was abundant sweet water. This fortress of Kitchener was simply a fortified place designed to protect the caravan road. Lubrous, as an identification of the site of Zoar, might well be equated with "ludicrous." A general who is great is not therefore a reliable archaeologist.

When yet far from our camping-place, at our approach an old castle had caught our eyes—and filled us with hope. Kesr Et-Tubah, the Arabs call it, which name is nothing more illuminating than "The Brick Castle." Such it proved to be; there are the ruins of a great mill, tradition says a sugar mill, which is probably correct. A fine stone aqueduct which brought the water down from the river may still be traced, and the mill-race that carried the water directly to the wheels is still to be seen. This mill site is at the edge of a considerable tell. This heap of ruins is regarded, and has been regarded for centuries, as the Arabic Zoar, a flourishing city in the great Arabic period. Perhaps the Crusaders built the mill, but Arabic civilization also had here a great development, for nearly all the ruins are Arabic, with also a few traces of Byzantine occupation.

"All the rivers run into the Sea." So we set out to follow this beautiful little river near our camp, down to where it loses itself in the Salt Sea, to learn what further discoveries might be made along its course. The course was northwest, toward a point near the centre of this lower end of the Sea. The channel was wide and very rocky. We set off on foot and soon saw things. The river ran for a time through green fields of wheat and timothy and by orchards and vineyards with many a thrifty but troublesome thorn bush. Then there were dura fields, and finally canebrakes of giant rushes. The tanglewood jungle, so suggestive of wild things, soon turned the suggestiveness into reality.

We exploded some hoary old legends about this fabled region. It has been said, "No wing ever fanned the air, no fin ever cut the water, and no life is round about the Dead Sea." When we came to the mouth of the river we found millions of little fish swimming about in the edge of the sea. I suppose that in the depths of the Sea, where the water is saturated with salt, fish do not exist, but there are certainly plenty of them where the fresh water comes in. Then, as Dr. Albright and I stumbled among the driftwood along the shore and among the lagoons, there was a great splashing and a whir of wings, and a flock of great ducks rose and flew out *over the sea. They* evidently had no aversion to the waters of the sea.

As we went on along a sandbar I exclaimed: "Look at those tracks! I suppose you know what it is that makes a track like that—one foot immediately in front of another? That was a cat; not a lion, but a tiger or a leopard or a wildcat." Presently another track not so large joined that one, and then there were added a whole bevy of little tracks. Evidently that whole cat family, tom-cat and tabby cat and all the kittens, were out for a picnic, and we had no desire to attend that picnic.

As we went back through the jungle we kept a sharp watch on every tree, lest a cat would come down on our heads. The next day when near a tree I heard a "hiss!" I sprang back, looking up to see that cat coming down on me. But it was not there. I then looked about for an adder that hisses also, but did not find it. Yet something hissed. Evidently there is life not only in the sea and the air, but in the jungle round about the sea, and that legend about the absolute lifelessness of this region has gone the way of many other legends —and that, even if we had not been also wading through almost tropical foliage.

On our way back to camp two other heaps of ruined cities were found, one of them with a large reservoir well plastered for the storing of water for irrigation purposes. The fine stone aqueduct which led the water of the river into the reservoir could still be traced for some distance. But here again were Arab remains, perhaps a little Byzantine, but nothing earlier. None of these tells, in this region around the camp, marks the site of the Cities of the Plain.

Next morning we were early in the saddle to ride to the southern end of the Plain. As we looked down to the Plain, dim in the distance, I said to Professor Day, our geologist, "Do you see that dark belt around the valley a little distance from the Sea?"

"Yes," said he, "I have been looking at that."

"Do you know what that means?"

"Yes; it means there is a rise in the ground

PITCHING TENTS TOWARD SODOM 63

there, and the thorn bushes give that dark appearance."

"Yes," said I, "we knew that was there before we came down here."

Sharp as a pistol shot came the question of a scientist, "How did you know that?"

"Because the Sea is rising at the northern end and, of course, finding its level everywhere. But water in a basin does not rise, if it can run over the edge. As the water in this basin is rising, we knew it *could not run over the edge*. That is to say, it has reached the high ground all around the Sea."

"I guess you are right."

By the eye we had noted a sharp rise in the ground; by the barometer it was found to be from fifty to one hundred feet, a very short distance back from the edge of the Plain occupied by the Sea. Here was a discovery which was indeed only the verification of what we knew must be the fact, yet it was one of the most important discoveries in establishing the history of the Cities of the Plain. Its full significance will appear as we go along in our researches.

After two hours' riding to the south we were able to look back upon the Sea almost due north. Instead of a glassy Sea from shore to shore, this lower part of the Sea appeared as a sea with a fringe, like a swamp with a fringe of cat-tails around it; only these cat-tails were dead and bleached trees; the fringe was a submerged forest. There were trees little and big, from mere saplings to trees a foot in diameter. It was a ghost of a forest once living and green, now dead and blasted a ghostly white by the salt. In places this submerged forest was seen to extend out a mile from the shore on the eastern side and somewhat less from the western side of this narrow arm of the Sea at the southern end.

Here we perceived not only that the Sea *is* rising, as we have already noted, but that it *has been* rising. Certainly within a hundred years, perhaps less by a half, this submerged forest on each side of the Sea stood upon dry ground where the trees grew to their present size. Thus for fifty years the Sea has been rising, yet rising very slowly, because it could still run over at this lower edge. Now it is rising rapidly because it cannot run over any more until it has risen very much. What causes the Sea either to rise or to run over the edge we shall presently see.

More beautiful streams of water were found at this lower end of the Plain, and more Bedouin, with their scant irrigation, and cultivation, and more ruins of a civilization that is dead and gone. Here was a mill with an aqueduct and evidence of an advanced efficiency. But here also were chiefly Arabic remains, perhaps a little Byzantine, but of the ancient Canaanite civilization not a trace. So we turn our horses' heads toward home, taking a short-cut on an inner circle of the shore, across the mud flats of the overflow at the time of the spring freshet of the Jordan. At one place we came near being bogged in the quicksands. And where the waters had stagnated in a little pool there was a swampy smell for a few rods, a mere suggestion of the horrid miasma so much exploited by visitors to this region.

I have said that we determined to comb this whole region for evidence, so the next day we set off on a real combing expedition, six hours of mountain climbing over the foothills of the mountains of Moab, to see if by any possibility ruins of the old civilization of the days of Sodom might be found on that high ground. We found one old castle guarding the pass, saw some most sublime mountain gorges and precipices, and I got into such hair-raising situations on the edge of the precipice that Dr. Albright said he held his breath lest I should go over and be lost in the chasm below. But the only thing we found that day that was memorable was an appetite. Six hours' climbing in the pure mountain air, with only bread and eating-chocolate for lunch, sent us home ravenous.

Our search of the Plain here was finished. We had ridden and walked up and down and round and round, but we had not seen the Cities of the Plain. The evidence, however, was seen to converge toward a certain point near the centre of this shallow water at the lower end of the Sea. The rivers all run toward that point. All the inhabitancy of the Plain, from Byzantine and Arabic and Crusader times down to the Bedouin and the soldiers and our own selves, has always been along these water courses. Where else would it be? for water is a prime necessity, and in this dry climate no cisterns are practicable. Were then any of these ruins now visible here the site of the ancient cities? No potsherds of their civilization had been found.

We determined to make soundings to find, if possible, the missing link of evidence. We arranged with the Bedouin Sheik for help in digging, to avoid their inveterate suspicion that all archaeologists are treasure seekers. We sounded down to the virgin sand and gravel. Not a trace of that early civilization was found; the ruins here now visible and so often described as the ruins of the Cities of the Plain are of a period two thousand

PITCHING TENTS TOWARD SODOM 67

years later. Some of these ruins do most probably mark the site of medieval Zoar, but nothing earlier.

The mission link was still missing. We go now to seek it.

LETTER SIX:
CAMP AT GHOR-EL-MEZRA'AH, MOAB

It was with something of regret that we struck our green tents at Ghor-Es-Safieh and left its sparkling canals, its white-tented guard and its black-tented Bedouin camp, its pleasant green fields, its gorgeous mountain views and its celestial sunsets. The ride up north was a pleasant continuance of interesting things that surrounded all our researches here, except that the gorgeous red sandstone gave way somewhat to a yellowish clay as we approached the foothills that rise east from the Lisan.

The Lisan, the "tongue," is just that. It is a kind of promontory that juts out from the eastern toward the western mountains, those of Judaea, and almost cuts the Sea in two. Anciently it manifestly separated the Great Sea to the north of it from the low plain to the south of it, and almost cut the great gorge of the Jordan Valley in two, leaving but a narrow, deep passageway between the northern part of the present Sea and the Plain that lay south of it.

68   EXPLORATIONS AT SODOM

One of the interesting things, here in the Orient, is that every now and then one finds himself in the footsteps of the Romans, actually going along an old Roman road. As we rode along that morning through mile after mile of the green oasis, or of the unbroken wild desert with the gravel and sand on the one hand, and the fields of wheat and grass, or the ever-intruding thorn bushes on the other, suddenly we became conscious that we were again on a made road. There, on the right hand, still holding its head up, was an old Roman milestone. The old Roman road! it ran up and down this plain at the edge of the mountain desert land. There was nothing specially significant in the road itself, for the Romans were everywhere in this land, but when a branch ran off to the left, right down the centre of the Lisan to the point where it reaches the narrow, deep gorge on the western side, the road suddenly became very significant.

The Romans did not build roads to nowhere. That road led down to a bridge or a ford or a ferry, or simply to a continuation of the road itself right across to the western side of the valley. Arabs of Kerak have told Père Vincent that they still remember a ford at that place. Thus again we have come upon evidence that the Sea was formerly at a lower

PITCHING TENTS TOWARD SODOM 69

level than now and did not cover this lower Plain. At most, the large portion of the Sea now to the south of Lisan was then of very narrow dimensions, as was indicated by the submerged forests.

Our new camp was by another little river, Seil-ed-Dra'a, by which the rushing sweet waters came down from the red sandstone hills of Moab and turned the Plain into a green oasis. The black tents of the Arabs were here also, and the Bedouin women baked bread for us, thin and black and dirty, but bread. They sold us eggs also, "this year's crop."

Director Albright was sending a man to buy eggs on one occasion and handed him a *mejidi*, a Turkish coin worth nearly a dollar.

"Oh," said the man, "I cannot buy eggs with mejidis; I must buy one egg from one woman, and two eggs from another woman, and I must have small money."

They sold us also one of their tough old hens, half-broiled it over their little fires; and then after we had stewed it a long time, we were able to imagine we had eaten a chicken dinner.

At the port Mezra'ah, the port of Kerak, the harbor-master—if he can be dignified with so high-sounding a name—was a young Arab of high rank, a sort of nobleman. He received us with ceremonies becoming his rank. After many salaams and much hand-shaking, a servant appeared with a bowl of warm milk, "a lordly dish" it was; whether the milk was cow's milk, or goat's milk or sheep's milk or was from the donkeys or the camels or the horses, they did not say—and I do not say. Probably my quizzical expression betrayed my thoughts, for Dr. Albright passed close by me, and said in English *sotto voce,* "Drink it; it is a ceremony." I drank, and we cemented our friendship in ——'s milk.

How beautiful the fields and the fig orchards and the Sea! And there is the motor-boat from the port of Jericho. How easily one little touch of civilization, even the chug, chug of a motor-boat, brings us right into civilization again with a bang. It is suggestive of automobiles and electric lights and everything that one can get by touching a button or stepping on the gas. Oh, the artificialness of civilized life! No more now will I carry hard-boiled eggs in my pocket with my Baedeker. But we are here to find that missing link of evidence, and must not give way to frivolous meditations.

That motor-boat, however, has to do with the story. We hired it for a day—and incidentally for about fifty dollars—for a search of the great shallow part of the Sea below the Lisan. Cruising on the Dead Sea is rather

PITCHING TENTS TOWARD SODOM 71

unusual, even among romantic explorations. In a few years it will be a favourite sport of the globe-trotters. This particular boat was not very luxurious, but the cruise was; the deep blue of the Sea, the marvellous colouring of the mountains on the east and on the west, and the strange fascination that the memory of the great tragedy throws over one, all make cruising on the Dead Sea unique.

We were a jolly company, including the young harbor-master; we invited him to show our genuine fraternal attitude. There must be no Nordic uppishness in dealing with these Ishmaelites of the desert; they have plenty of uppishness of their own. So we all lunched together. The lunch was not elaborate, but our Dead Sea appetite was. Our steward had provided Bedouin thin tough loaves and canned baked beans for the day, with pasteboard plates for the beans. We discarded the plates as entirely an unnecessary refinement; instead we folded a section of the thin tough bread, spooned a liberal supply of beans into that pocket and gormandized on that fat sandwich. The beans were excellent; the bread about the texture and much the flavor of a hot-water bottle, and as tough as—— Well, I chewed a long time, and thought to myself, "That bread is certainly tough." Then I discovered that for some time I had been chewing upon the leather chin strap of my sun hat. I had not noticed any difference in the taste!

We turn our prow toward that sugar-loaf mountain on the west coast gleaming silvery white in the distance. It is Jebul Usdum, the mountain of Sodom, and its silver hue is no hallucination, but the out-gleam of its very nature. It is not really a mountain, being only about five hundred feet high; and measured as we measure mountains, from the sea level, paradoxical as it sounds, it also is really a hole in the ground, for the top of that mountain is still seven hundred feet below sea-level. Its silvery sheen arises from the fact that the great base of that mountain is a stratum of rock salt almost absolutely pure, a hundred and fifty feet thick and stretching for some miles along the west shore of the Sea. In the seams of the stratum and in the clay above, there is the marl mixed with free sulphur, of which I have spoken.

We landed on a ledge of the shore, and went into a cave whose sides are gleaming rock salt. The water here is very shallow. Lynch, of the United States Navy, found it only from a foot to seventeen and a half feet, in 1857. As the Sea had risen enough since that time to take in those submerged forests, it is probably now twenty-five feet in the deepest part here.

PITCHING TENTS TOWARD SODOM 73

Our boat anchored two or three rods from shore, and the Arabs carried us to shore and back. Coming back to deck, my porter stepped in a hole. Lincoln once said, in reply to a question, that he thought a man's legs ought to be long enough to reach from his body to the ground. When that Arab stepped in the hole I discovered that my legs reached from my body down a considerable distance into the Dead Sea! My puttees protected me a little, but my feet and my knees were very wet. The engineers made a place, in the heat of the gasoline engine, in which I dried my clothes until they were incrusted over with salt, somewhat like Lot's wife of old.

We landed, on the return, about four miles from camp. Our muleteers, by some misunderstanding, had gone back to camp with the horses. It was ten o'clock at night—and the trail was almost undiscoverable even by day. Besides, here and there we had to pass through water. One of the young fellows grabbed me up bodily and carried me over, despite my protests. Then we borrowed a lantern and secured a guide, and I said, "Come on now; four miles is not much of a walk." They would not have it so. Somewhere they got one horse, and insisted that I ride. I absolutely refused. But the director said, "Ride this horse, out of respect to the sentiments of the staff." So I had to yield, and mount that steed and follow humbly.

I may now confess that my protests were not all from humility. The stirrups were about a foot too short, and the saddle was very hard. For one hour I held on as best I could while my feet dangled and swung. Walking would have been a luxury, but, "out of respect for the sentiments of the staff," I was not entirely comfortable for some days afterwards.

But that day yielded something more than salt mountains and sentimental experiences.

As, when there is not soot found in a chimney, it is certain there has been no fire in that chimney, for fire leaves soot; so civilization, like fire, leaves soot—unmistakable remains. Père Mallon, scouring the edge of the mountain for flints and stone artifacts, that very morning of our day upon the Sea, had come upon some graves which the Arabs had opened in search for treasure. We knew that in graves was the place to look for the evidence that we sought but had not yet found.

Opening graves is a dangerous procedure among the Arabs. They are exceedingly sensitive about the disturbing of a grave, if an Arab is buried in it, and who can be sure who *may* be in a grave, until it is opened? But here were some graves which they themselves had opened, and here was the longed-for pottery of the Early Bronze Age, the time of Abraham and of Sodom.

Having shown that the traditional sites do not show the civilization of the time of the Cities of the Plain, we were then face to face with the question, Are such evidences of civilization of that Age to be found anywhere on the Plain? This is the finally determining quest, for the Biblical story cannot be authenticated unless evidence of that civilization can be found. Without it, history would not be disproved, but would always have a question mark after it. Of the greatest interest, as well as for light it sheds upon the culture of Sodom and Gomorrah, was our discovery, beside this group of graves, of a vast open-air settlement of the Early Bronze Age (third millennium B.C.) at Bab-ed-Dra'a, five hundred feet above the Dead Sea, on the road from Mezra'a to Kerak. The settlement contained a fortress over a thousand feet in length, surrounded by a massive wall and revêtment, the former ten to fifteen feet thick. The latter, some fifteen feet high, where sufficiently preserved to enable one to determine the height.

Just south of the fortress was this extensive open-air settlement, consisting of hearths and enclosures, over which booths were probably erected. A few minutes' walk to the east of the fortress, on the edge of the open-air settlement just described, is a group of six sacred pillars, or *masseboth,* with the fragments of a seventh, all prostrate on the ground. The limestone monoliths must have been dragged for miles to be set up here as *masseboth.* Around the edges of the settlement are numerous graves, still nearly all unopened.

Since the finds show that the spot was long occupied, while the absence of a deposit of débris, either inside or outside the fortress, shows that it was not consecutively occupied for any length of time, the only conclusion is that we have here a kind of early Canaanite Gilgal, to which annual pilgrimages were made to celebrate a feast, probably either a spring festival somewhat analogous to the Passover, or a harvest festival like the Feast of Booths (Succoth). Naturally, the rites and practises were corrupt and heathenish to a degree, as we may safely suppose from the Biblical accounts of Sodom and Baal-peor, both in the vicinity.

Because the inhabitants of the highlands of Moab at that time were nomads, as conclusively proved by our later investigations there, and the massive fortress with its revêtment, reminding one of that of Jericho, probably belonged to a sedentary population, it seems

PITCHING TENTS TOWARD SODOM 77

highly probable that our sanctuary was visited mainly by pilgrims from the Cities of the Plain, rather than by nomads from the highlands, who would not think of building a fortress and thus acting at variance with their usual customs. The fortress was, then, intended primarily as a protection to the visitors at the shrine, who might otherwise be in danger of an attack from the hills.

From the inside of the fortress and the open-air settlement to the south of it, we collected several thousand flint artifacts, besides several boxes full of pottery, mostly characteristic sherds. The artifacts consist mainly of knives, some very fine, of scrapers for hides, of awls, and sickle edges, etc. The pottery is a very representative collection of types from the Early Bronze Age and the beginning of the Middle Bronze Age, and covers several centuries, perhaps nearly a thousand years, from the middle of the third millennium to not later than the eighteenth century. It has been examined by Père Vincent and Phythian-Adams, at present the foremost experts on the subject, and they agree with the conclusions reached by the members of the expedition.

The pottery is mostly handmade, but is of good quality, and consists of several types: Large plates or platters with an inverted rim, red in colour and highly polished or burnished;

78 EXPLORATIONS AT SODOM

bowls with wavy ledge handles, small water decanters with vertical loop handles. Nearly all have flat bottoms. In some tombs which had been opened by the Arabs a number of nearly complete vessels were found, besides a quantity of human skulls and bones, a collection of which was made by Professor Day and will be submitted to a leading anthropologist for examination. One loop handle picked up was rudely modelled in the form of a human head, but the normal skulls found in the grave show that the potter had little anatomical skill.

Most suggestive is the fact that the evidence of pottery sets the end of the settlement at Bab-ed-Dra'a at about the time when Biblical sources place the catastrophe of the Cities of the Plain. This coincidence can hardly be accidental. We therefore seem to be justified in supposing that Bab-ed-Dra'a was one of the sacred places, probably the Great High Place, of the inhabitants of Sodom and Gomorrah, to which they made annual pilgrimages, and where they may have practised nameless rites, the nature of which had better not be surmised, in view of our other information about Canaanite religion. The distance from the settlement on the Plain was short; our shrine would be about twelve miles in a straight line from ancient Zoar, if our approximate localizations

PITCHING TENTS TOWARD SODOM 79

are correct, and hardly more than five miles from the nearest town on the Plain.

Here were the sure marks of the Canaanite civilization of that age, and sure proof that such civilization had ceased from that time on. Nowhere is there a trace of civilization of any kind again until we come to Byzantine times, except it be the cryptic reference of Ezekiel to the return of the captivity of Sodom, which probably means only that this utter desolation which had then lasted so long would at last be relieved, as it is likely soon to be. The silence of Scripture during these long centuries is no more significant than is the silence in this lore of pottery.

We had now found all we hoped to find, but, as so often, Providence sends more than we hope or ask. Lot went up into the mountain when he was afraid to stay even in Zoar. The civilization that arose in that land is, then, attributed to him as the progenitor. Critics have sometimes stoutly insisted that there was no such civilization at that date in Moab.

However, I found an inscription of Rameses the Great at Luxor temple in 1908, in which he boasts of having made conquest of Moab. This certifies the history of Moab at the time of the Exodus. Then, a few days after the discovery of the old civilization at Bab-ed-

Dra'a, there was found at Ader in Moab, a Moabite temple. It was similar in some respects to the temple of Solomon, though smaller and ruder. The pottery connected with it showed it to be of the age immediately succeeding the destruction of Sodom, 1800–1600 B.C. Thus we have scientific evidence complete of the civilization represented as immediately succeeding the going of Lot to Moab.

The missing link of evidence had now been found. The story was complete, and we were ready to gather up the results and to learn all that is known now from all sources. We did not find anything so sensational as Tut-Ankh-Amen's tomb, but we found scientific evidence of more value in the study of the Holy Land, and especially in furnishing the historical sanctions of the Biblical narrative, than would have been the discovery of a king's crown.

II

CIVILIZATION IN THE JORDAN VALLEY

LETTER SEVEN:
IN THE SHADE OF A THORN-TREE, AT SODOM

WE must be careful as we walk under the trees in this valley, careful lest we step on a great thorn. This is the thorniest region imaginable; scarcely anything grows out of the ground that does not grow prickles of some sort. So take this camp chair, and do not sit on the ground.

Move forward also, just a little farther into the shade, lest the sun behind us, as we face north for our study of the Valley, strike on the back of your neck. It is not mere fashion of the desert that these Bedouins wrap the long cloth of their turbans in a thick coil high on the neck or bundle up their heads even in hot weather. It is inherited wisdom of the ages. The sun is an enemy in this land that must be faced, if possible; one might better carelessly turn his back on a lion of the desert than let even the winter sun strike at the base of the brain.

Now we are safe and comfortable, and fitted into the conditions of the primitive life of the patriarchs, or of those Judges who judged "under a tree."

If we would take a look back into the civilization of this Jordan Valley, we must first take a look around about us in the Valley itself. We have come down from the house in which the world lives into the cellar of this the dwelling-place of the human race. The upper story is twelve hundred and fifty feet above us. The place where the world lives and labours and studies and enjoys itself is away up yonder, where the red sandstone of the mountains of Moab tower above us.

Strange dark things are to be found in cellars. No wonder we have here the disappointing apples of Sodom giving us little more than a puff of dust, and poisonous melons which were "death in the pot" for the prophets of old. Venomous adders are here, also, and spiteful scorpions.

The walls of this subterranean place present, also, amazing things like the caverns of Luray. That gleaming precipice along the west side of the Sea is the great salt-bed that underlies the mountain of Sodom and likewise underlies the story of the destruction of the

CIVILIZATION IN JORDAN VALLEY 83

Cities. That ghastly yellow marl overlying the salt is the natural home of the sulphur whence came the burning brimstone that destroyed the plain.

The eastern walls of this cellar are red as blood, like the red of Edom and of those freakish rocks that portal the Gateway of the Garden of the Gods at Pike's Peak. Here is the ash-heap of this cellar of the world.

Yet here, on the floor of this cellar, is a tropical garden "even as the garden of the Lord." The sweet water of the red sandstone mountains waters it, the little runlets made by Bedouin hands distribute that water to the gardens and the fields and the orchards for a five-fold harvest year by year.

Despite the saltness of the Sea, this whole valley is thus well watered. The Jordan, the "descender," comes down to these depths from the very base of Great Hermon, eighty miles away, and brings the never-failing flood of the melting snows of the mountain, and pours it down into this deep-lying valley, this great rift in the crust of the earth. Straight as a line this deep gulch comes down between yonder mountains of Naphtali, Zebulon, Manasseh, Ephraim, little Benjamin, and Judah on the west, and the highland of Bashan and the Wall of Moab on the east. It is as a luxuriant sunken garden all the way until it ends at this Plain where we now sit under our thorn-tree a quarter of a mile below the place where the rest of the world lives.

This vision of the Valley prepares us to understand the beginnings of civilization here, and that, too, without a written record. Common-sense is the most absolutely universal characteristic which the continuity of nature has given the human race. Anthropologists and other folk who study the history of the race sometimes forget this. There is a theory about the beginnings of Semitic culture in the world that makes its homeland to be in the desert of Arabia, the fabled *Khedem,* the East, and would have the more verdant lands round about to be overrun periodically by excursions of these desert dwellers, the last of which excursions was the Mohammedan invasion. Now, about that theory:

If we were of those who began in the world, with *all the world before us,* its verdure, its fountains, its abundance for the possession of which there was no one to compete, would we go out and sit down in the middle of the desert, and that when nobody was chasing us? Would we leave this fruitful land toward the Great Sea and trek out into inhospitable Arabia? Not so; and no number of "excursions" which have actually taken place from Arabia *in later centuries* can satisfy common-

A GREAT GORGE IN THE MOUNTAINS OF MOAB

CIVILIZATION IN JORDAN VALLEY 85

sense that people with all the world before them would choose to begin in the most inhospitable place within reach.

This sidewise glimpse at a theory is not the digression it may seem to be; it has immediate application to the attractiveness of this sunken garden to the first inhabitants of Palestine. The earliest settlements were toward the north, they were coming down before the fierce north wind and—another manifestation of common-sense—were taking the course of least resistance down the easy valleys between the Lebanon and the Anti-Lebanon; and so from yonder at the foot of Hermon they were lured by the warmth and the verdure of this "sunken garden," and the occupation of the Jordan Valley began. The scene between Abram and Lot long afterwards is typical as well as historical; Lot was surely a man of common-sense, which when perverted becomes human selfishness that looks out for Number One.

As Lot stood on the great stony central ridge of the land, where indeed the stones must needs be heaped up into huge fencing walls in order to get room to cultivate the soil, that prospect did not hold much lure compared with the narrow green ribbon of the Jordan Valley three thousand feet below. He pitched his tent toward Sodom. So, when the first dwellers in this land stood at the foot

86 EXPLORATIONS AT SODOM

of Hermon and viewed the limestone backbone of the central ridge and then looked down this verdant, fertile, well-watered sunken garden stretching away south in the warm sunlight, they also took the course of least resistance and came down this valley.

This is not only exactly what we would expect, it is also what happened. The first considerable civilization of the land, not to say its first inhabitancy, was in this Jordan Valley. "The vast majority of ancient sites in this region were already inhabited early in the Bronze Age, and most of them have since been abandoned. In fact, as we shall see, the population of the Jordan Valley in the third millennium B.C. must have been greater than it has ever been since."[1] In fact, the first inhabitants had been coming down this valley a long time before they came to the foot of Hermon and looked down to this spot where we sit in the shade and trace their movements. For this Jordan Valley is not merely the valley of the Jordan River. That little river is but an incident along the

[1] Dr. W. F. Albright, *Annual Volume of the American Schools of Oriental Research*, 1926, p, 13. My colleague has most generously placed all the materials of this illuminating and exhaustive discussion of the civilization of the Jordan Valley at my service, and I gladly avail myself of his painstaking labours. For many of the other library references in this chapter I am also indebted to him, the books not being available at this writing.

CIVILIZATION IN JORDAN VALLEY 87

long way of the valley. The valley in its whole length is known in geology as the Miocene rift.

Away back in the history of world-making some stupendous contortion of nature cracked open the crust of the earth from north to south, from far away north, at shortest from upper Syria, down the Jordan Valley, on across the Sinai peninsula and lengthwise of the eastern side of the Continent of Africa, and for all we know under the waters of the sea to the south pole! This Jordan Valley at the Dead Sea is the deepest part of the crack, though the smallest part of its length. Professor Day, the geologist of our staff says:

"During the Jurassic and Cretaceous periods much of what we now call the Near East was part of an enlarged Mediterranean which covered Syria and Palestine and much of Egypt and Arabia and Asia Minor, and also stretched eastward over the Caucasus and Himalaya mountains to the Pacific. It was in the early part of the Tertiary Period that extensive portions of the bottom of this sea were lifted up and became land. The movement was very slow. Here and there great wrinkles or folds were produced, constituting the Lebanon and other mountains. These were not simple folds, but were complicated with subordinate folds and frequent fractures. Such fractures are nearly vertical cracks or fissures, sometimes of slight extent, sometimes extending for miles and of great depth. There is often a differential movement between the two sides of the fissure, constituting a fault.

"A series of tremendous faults marks the line of the 'Arabah, the Dead Sea, the Jordan, and the Sea of Galilee, from which it extends north by Lake Hulah, and thence, passing to the west side of Mount Hermon, follows the plain of Coele-Syria between Lebanon and Anti-Lebanon, and possibly is further indicated by the River Orontes in north Syria. Moreover, it is considered by eminent geologists that this series, which, for the sake of brevity, may be called the Jordan Valley Fault, is only a continuation of the great African rift valley, which, beginning with Lake Nyassa south of the equator, includes Lakes Tanganyika, Albert Edward, and Albert, while an eastern branch runs through Lake Rodolph, and then, passing between Abyssinia and Somaliland, follows the line of the Red Sea and the Gulf of 'Akabah to the 'Arabah, and thence to the Dead Sea and the Jordan" (*Bibliotheca Sacra*, July, 1924, page 264).

The entire length of this Jordan part of the great rift, from the foot of Hermon to the comparative highland that closes the lower end of this Plain of Sodom where we sit, is one hundred miles, and its greatest depth, measured from the same point to the bottom of the Dead Sea, is more than three thousand feet. It is doubtful if the early inhabitants had any way of determining either the heights of the mountains or the depths of the Valley in comparison with sea-level, but the physical appearance was the same to their eyes then as to our eyes now. They went into the depths here knowingly.

A knowledge of other conditions of life in

CIVILIZATION IN JORDAN VALLEY 89

the land, then, is not so difficult now as it might at first appear. There has been much speculation, some of it in the name of scientific research. A little common-sense attention to the things that can be seen exposes a large part of the speculations to ridicule. As Dr. Albright [2] points out:

The ruins of the ancient cities, tells, as the mounds are now called, are exactly where one would expect to find them. There can thus have been no great change in the conformation of the land or the location and course of streams of water by an action of earthquake or any process of de-forestation. Evidently all these things which condition life *were much the same then as now*. The number of tells great and small, and the enormous size of some of them, makes it plain that the population of the Jordan Valley in the third millennium, B.C. was not only greater than it is now, but greater than it has ever been from that day to this, not excepting even the commercial centre of population around the Lake of Galilee, in the days of our Lord.

The present distressing climatic influences, and especially the prevalence of malaria in the Valley now, there is good reason to believe arises not from any real change in climate,

[2] *Annual Volume of the American Schools of Oriental Research*, July, 1924, pages 13–14.

but from the neglect of the drainage and irrigating ditches. This is exactly the reverse of the change that has come to the region of Panama by proper drainage which has abolished the breeding places of the malarial mosquito. There is no reason to believe that the ancients in this Valley understood these hygienic measures, but excellent reason for believing that they attended to drainage for purposes of cultivation, and the attendant undesigned result was the salubriousness of the whole region.

Before passing in review the principal ruins in the Jordan Valley it is necessary for the quieting of the apprehensiveness of the uninitiated, for whom this book is written, to explain somewhat carefully the fundamental principles of archaeological science in Bible Lands. The popular notion concerning archaeology as a real science has been, to say the least, only tolerant and sometimes intolerant. Most people have been wondering if the archaeologist knows and knows that he knows, or if he only makes a more or less clever guess. The inclination has been decidedly toward the guess and without too much emphasis upon the cleverness of it. It will clear the atmosphere very much if we make plain at the outset that archaeology in Bible Lands is a real

CIVILIZATION IN JORDAN VALLEY 91

science, as trustworthy as any other historical science.

The beginning of this science in Bible Lands dates from the coming thither, about a quarter of a century ago, of Professor, now Sir, William Flinders Petrie, for exploration work. He brought with him the experience and observations of nearly a third of a century of exploration in Egypt. He had done more digging in that land than any other person, and almost more than all others put together. He pointed out and clearly established three things which are now the organizing norms of archaeological science in Bible Lands.

He perceived that the débris, ruined cities, in Bible Lands lies in layers, as geological layers anywhere and as may be seen everywhere in stone quarries. The reason for this is that there was no street-cleaning department in the city government in those old cities. If each Roman swept in front of his own door, each Canaanite swept things out in front of his door, and allowed them to accumulate there. When it got up to the level of the door sill—well, he put in a new floor, and raised the roof—but he did not clear the street. Then, when an earthquake, or an enemy, threw down the houses and they came to rebuild, they did not clear away the rubbish, but levelled it about a bit and built right on top of it. Thus a tell today represents accumulated cities one on top of the other and each in its own distinct layer. The upper layers trickle down a little into those underneath, but it is easy to separate the débris. Sometimes a tell has three, four, seven, eight, even as many as thirteen layers each representing a successive city.

A second discovery of this distinguished archaeologist was that each distinct civilization in the layers of débris had its own distinctive pottery, quite as distinctive as is Rookwood, Delft, and Dolton of fashionable tableware among ourselves, as distinctive indeed as Etruscan ware is of a certain age in Italy or Aegean ware in Greece. Wherever in Palestine a certain layer of civilization is reached in the ruins of any city, the characteristic pottery of that age is always found, and wherever in the ruins we find the distinctive pottery of any age, it is certain that we have to do there with the civilization of that age.

These two discoveries are epochal, but not definitely determinative; they differentiated the various Ages distinctly, but did not date any of them. But Professor Petrie was an Egyptologist. And in all ages of the civilization of Palestine Egyptians had been present bringing with them their own pottery and

CIVILIZATION IN JORDAN VALLEY 93

amulets, their own gods and goddesses and inscriptions. These Professor Petrie could date very accurately to the period to which they belonged. In dating these things he dated also the layer, and any particular level in a layer, in which they might be found. Other relics also could sometimes be dated.

These three discoveries made archaeology in Palestine a real historical science. In large measure the same touchstones may be used throughout Bible Lands, and especially in Babylonia. The data thus furnished enables the discoverer today to arrange his finds in chronological order and to date them with satisfactory accuracy, though not always to a year and a day.

Two great ages of civilization in Bible Lands are indicated by the data, the Bronze Age and the Iron Age, more popularly described as Canaanite civilization and Israelite civilization, because the Bronze Age, 2500-1300 B.C., covers the Canaanite occupation and the Early Iron Age, 1300-600 B.C., marks the time from the incoming of the Israelites and the Philistines onward to the end of the Early Iron Age, when Israelite occupation was rudely broken by Nebuchadnezzar. These general divisions are broken up into subdivisions: Early Bronze Age to about 1800 B.C., the Middle Bronze Age to 1600 B.C., and the Late

94 EXPLORATIONS AT SODOM

Bronze Age to 1300 B.C. And the Early Iron Age is subdivided into Early Iron one, two and three.

With these principles and divisions of Biblical Archaeology in mind, we are ready now to survey the civilization of the Jordan Valley from the earliest times down to the age when took place those events to study which we have come to this place. This survey will bring us to the Great Break in the civilization, that tragic catastrophe recorded in Holy Writ as the destruction of Sodom and Gomorrah and marked in both sacred and secular history and in the pottery record by a ghastly vacancy of twenty-five hundred years. It will contribute much to clearness to note at the outset that we have to deal wholly with the Bronze Ages, the Early, the Middle and the Late Bronze, and for the spot where we sit under our thorn-tree, only the Early Bronze Age. This lower end of the Valley *has no Early Iron Age history at all.*

Now, as we sit in the shade of a thorn-tree, and in the sunlight of a brighter civilization, we may take a look along this deep valley as through a long telescope and get a far-away vision of the early civilization of the Valley.

Yonder, at the foot of the Great Hermon, eighty miles away in the length of the land, and near 5,000 years away in the history of

CIVILIZATION IN JORDAN VALLEY 95

the world, we get a vision of a straggling, struggling population pushing its way down the Great Rift, shrinking from the cold wintry blasts of the north and dropping quietly with a sigh of content into the shelter of this deep sunny valley. Far along in the history of Israel that beginning place of the civilization of the Jordan Valley was called Dan, "formerly" it had been Laish, as the Hebrews spelled it, Lawis as the Egyptian scribes spelled it.[3]

There they built their first city, round about which they lived and laboured. The earliest city, it is evident, was later moved a little way, for that earliest city presents now only the pottery of the Early Bronze Age. The subsequent course of history in the Valley is easily traced. Whether it be bad or good, it goes inevitably on; for, once this Valley was entered upon, it was certain to be followed down to its depths.

The downward course in history, as in morals, is the course of least resistance, so easy and so all but inevitable. The facts show that in this case it became actual; the pottery reveals that the people of the Early Bronze Age back to the beginning of that Age, perhaps even into the latter part of the fourth millennium B.C., pushed down this Valley to

[3] *Palestinian List of Thothmes III*, number 31. Muller's *Egyptological Researches*, 1906, page 1.

the end. So we have tell after tell in a line down the river: Tell en Na' meh (The northern Yenoamam, though probably not as it seems to me, the one mentioned in the Israel tablet of Merenptah); Tell Abil (Abel-beth-Maachah, 1 Kings 15:20); Tell el-Oreimeh (Chinnereth).

The beautiful site of Tell Hum, Capernaum, they passed by, strange to say, for the pottery at the ruins there shows the place was not occupied until the end of ancient Israelite history, in the Hellenistic Age. Nor were these early settlers much interested in the hot springs that made Tiberius famous in Roman times. Health resorts are always most used by people who come to them, not by the people who live near them. So the Bronze Age people passed the hot springs by, and built what was probably their greatest city at the place where the Jordan leaves the Lake of Galilee in its downward course. At this place are still the very extensive ruins of Beit Yerah (later, Scythopolis of the Greeks and Romans).

The great accumulation of débris with potsherds of the Early Bronze Age indicate that these early settlers were not blind to the commercial and industrial advantages of the situation at the foot of the Lake near the ford of the Jordan, the great crossroads of the land. Far down the course of history the

CIVILIZATION IN JORDAN VALLEY 97

Romans also built the industrial emporium, Tarachaea, near the same spot.

Next below the Lake, Beth Shean (modern Beisan) on the river Jalud lifts up its towering height to guard the south side of the crossroads. Of less importance at first than Beth Yerah, it soon outstripped that place and continued to dominate the trade routes and the Plain of Esdraealon and the lower Jordan Valley long after Beth Yerah was forgotten. It divided with Gezer the Egyptian domination of Palestine and only fell to the Israelites in the days of David, while Gezer was not obtained, but by diplomacy in the days of Solomon.

From Beth Shean down the Valley the population was distributed into many small settlements, clinging to the mountain side, guarding important points, utilizing the abundant waters of the Jordan Valley again and again, down to the *kikkar,* the "great round," that broad plain of the Jordan that begins near where Jericho stands and encloses in its circle the Dead Sea and the Plain south of it. In addition to the waters of the Jordan the Great Round was watered by copious streams and fountains, Ain es-Sultan at Jericho, Wady Kelt, the traditional Brook Cherith, a little below, Ain Gedi on the west of the Dead Sea, the river Arnon on the east. The abundant waters of the three rivers from the Red Sandstone mountains of Moab also pour into the lower end of the Valley by the Cities of the Plain.

The ruins of ancient Jericho are still much of a puzzle. The remains so conspicuously in evidence there today are, of course, remains of later constructions of the city that has been destroyed many times. How often, who can say? However, the pottery tells the tale of the inhabitancy of the various cities here. Very soon after civilization came into the Valley, it came here, away back in the Early Bronze Age, and left its unmistakable tokens there to be found by Sellin and Watzinger. Of that early city little or nothing remains above ground. The report of the archaeologists and the record in Joshua agree in this. Moreover that is the way cities were destroyed in the olden days, much as the villages and towns in northern France were destroyed in the Great War. Whatever means may be used, destructive human ruthlessness accomplishes its purpose. The ruins of later cities have left a great accumulation at Jericho. Even at thirty feet, virgin soil was not found.[4]

The pottery shows that certainly in that early age, the time of Abraham and Lot and of Sodom and Gomorrah, and of the story just

[4] Sellin and Watzinger, *Jericho*, page 19.

CIVILIZATION IN JORDAN VALLEY 99

now so greatly interesting us, at Jericho, there was a formidable fortress city, the culmination there of that great civilization which had now stretched down from the foot of Hermon to this broad plain, the Great Round. Thence we drift with the flow of population down to this lower Plain where we are sitting in the shade of our friendly thorn-tree.

We must turn now to the Biblical history and put round about us a knowledge of this region and what happened here of which Holy Writ furnishes the only written record.

III

A TRAGIC STORY IN HISTORY AND PROPHECY

LETTER EIGHT:
IN THE SHADE OF A THORN-TREE, AT SODOM

FROM the fascinating story of the civilization of the Jordan Valley so graphically portrayed in the remains of antiquity, written, like messages from the old prophets, on potsherds, we must turn now to the tragic story recorded in history and prophecy that may bring before us the next scene in the unfolding drama of life in this Jordan Valley. That we may be undisturbed, we must escape from the chaffering of the muleteers round about our tents and the kitchen clatter within them.

So, with Bibles under our arms, we will betake us again to the inviting shade of our great thorn-tree by the gurgling waters that rush through the little runlets meandering over the Plain to irrigate the fields of the Bedouin below us. We will place our camp-chairs carefully in the spot of shade from the

A TRAGIC STORY 101

leafy top of the tree and pull down the back visor of our sun helmets, that the rays of the tropical sun may not by any possibility strike at the base of the brain as we again look north.

We will also carefully turn over all these flat stones about our feet to see that no treacherous scorpion is hiding underneath. We are in a very old world here, but are very new in it, and so must do very unusual things. Now we are all set for the tragic story.

The first historical reference to Sodom is that characteristically Bedouin story of the quarrelling and bartering of Abram and Lot on the great central ridge of the land from which we also set out to study the Plain. They had just come up from a none too successful sojourn in Egypt, where trickiness had nearly proved disastrous. It is not surprising to find family troubles cropping out. The humbling of Abram down in Egypt may have done him good, for he is most generous and straightforward here. Certainly the sanctity of his life is remarkably displayed in the pacific offer to Lot in the quarrel: "Is not the whole land before thee? Separate thyself, I pray thee, from me; if thou wilt take the left hand, then I will go to the right; or if thou wilt take the right hand, then I will go to the left" (Gen. 13:9).

102   EXPLORATIONS AT SODOM

The selfish shrewdness of Lot is equally apparent in his instant choice of the green valley below, instead of the stony ridge round about. So Lot "dwelt in the Cities of the Plain, and pitched his tent toward Sodom." This statement is most suggestive topographically; for, however many were the "Cities of the Plain" in which he dwelt, Sodom, toward which he "pitched his tent," must then have been *farthest away*. This directs our thought right down to this Plain, where we sit under the thorn-tree.

"But the men of Sodom were wicked and sinners before the Lord exceedingly" (Gen. 13:13). "And the Lord said, Because the cry of Sodom and Gomorrah is great, and because their sin is very grievous; I will go down and see whether they have done altogether according to the cry of it, which is come unto me; and if not, I will know" (Gen. 18:20–21).

And now the scene is laid away up yonder above Hebron, some thirty-five miles from where we sit. "And the men turned their faces from thence, and went toward Sodom: but Abraham stood yet before the Lord" (Gen. 18:22).

Then we witness a wonder only twice parallelled in the history of the world when Moses prayed for the people (Ex. 32:31–32), and when our Lord "went a little way and fell

A TRAGIC STORY

on his face and prayed saying, 'If it be possible, let this cup pass from me; nevertheless not my will, but thine be done'" (Matt. 26:39).

Not one of these three petitions was granted. We may wonder what would have happened, if Abraham had not stopped in his petition. Probably it is well always to stop, when the Lord withholds *faith to go on*. The doom of Sodom was prepared, and was not to be stopped.

We understand this as we follow "the men" down here to the Plain and read of the happenings at Sodom that evening. The story smells worse than the sulphur that fell next day. The conduct of the Sodomites explains the catastrophe to Sodom and the finality of the announcement of the angels, "The Lord hath sent us to destroy it." The men of Sodom mobbed the angels, and the sons-in-law of Lot mocked at the warning given them, and even Lot and his household were so reluctant that they had to be "laid hold of" by the hand and led away with the urgent injunction: "Escape for thy life; look not behind thee, neither stay thee in the Plain; escape to the mountain, lest thou be consumed."

Somewhere, not far away among these thorn-trees of the Plain close to the foot of the mountains of Moab, stood the little city of Zoar. Lot begged for it and for permission to stop there. How like sinners always, so reluctant to be saved! Later the fear entered into his soul, and he fled to the mountain. He found, as sinners always find in the end, that the Lord's advice is best.

Now, the divine hand that held in leash the doom of the Cities was loosed for the destruction of the "cities and the plain and everything that grew out of the ground." Salt and sulphur and fire! What could be more destructive of fertility. We only have a description of the scene that day from the standpoint of Abraham away up yonder on the mountain near Hebron. He could see only the smoke "as the smoke of a furnace."

Nobody at Sodom survived to tell the tragic tale. How much we would like to have Lot's account and the story of the people of Zoar! But probably the eyes of all were so filled with smoke, and their nostrils so offended by sulphur, that they could have told us but little. Six hundred years afterward Moses could still speak of the "overthrow of the cities," and record that "the whole land thereof is brimstone and salt and burning, that it is not sown, nor beareth, nor any grass groweth therein" (Deut. 29:23).

Six hundred years more pass over the place, and still Isaiah characterizes its desolateness

A TRAGIC STORY 105

thus: "It shall never be inhabited, neither shall it be dwelt in from generation to generation: neither shall the Arabian pitch tent there; neither shall the shepherds make their fold there" (Isa. 13:20).

From this time of the destruction onward, the very name of Sodom furnishes an appellation for unmentionable vileness, and the fate of Sodom a warning horror to flaunt in the face of impenitent sinners even from the lips of our Lord (Matt. 10:15, Luke 17:29). Twenty-eight times, by twelve different Biblical writers, including a quotation from our Lord Himself, these cities are held up to execration as a lurid warning to other peoples and nations who would escape the wrath of God.

When, now, we turn to take a look at the history of the Plain after the catastrophe, the horror of the catastrophe only is driven the deeper into our souls. The Plain has no history, to the end of the Biblical story. Only once is there perhaps a reference to the lower end of this Plain, toward the border of Edom as it impinges on the territory of Moab. When the three kings, Jehoram of Israel, Jehoshaphat of Judah and the king of Edom fought against Moab they passed by the edge of this Plain. But there is no hint of inhabitant, and the place itself was so dry and desolate that a miracle was needed to save the combined armies from death for lack of water.

Even the irrigation ditches *had to be made.* Then the Lord filled these trenches in some marvellous way, and the morning sun laid upon the water the blood red color of the sandstone mountains round about, and the enemy conceived the notion that the kings had fought among themselves and covered the ground with blood. No more certain evidence of the absolutely desert character of this region in those days could be imagined. A long description would be less convincing.

The tradition of this Plain that has lingered to recent times was at that time a reality; here was a dead land round about a dead sea, and harbouring the memory of a moral character that was dead and a stench in the nostrils of the whole world.

IV

UNSCIENTIFIC SPECULATIONS OF PILGRIMS AND TRAVELLERS

LETTER NINE:
UNDER THE SAME THORN-TREE

WE come now to the dark ages of Palestinian history, which curiously enough correspond in part to the dark ages in Europe. There, as in the Holy Land, the utter crushing out of the Jewish national life, and from this the diaspora which scattered the people of Israel throughout the world and most effectively ended the dominion of Jewish people in the Holy Land. There came then into the world the decline and fall of the Roman Empire and with it the ancient civilization of the world. Then followed the incoming of the Huns and the Vandals from the North, the upcoming of the Mohammedan invasion of Europe, the rise and rule of the Saracens, and then the decline of the Arabic civilization. With these kaleidoscopic changes not only did the history of the Land of Promise fail, it came at last that the land itself had to be re-discovered.

108 EXPLORATIONS AT SODOM

All these dark ages of world history we must, here at Sodom and Gomorrah, add to the Great Break in the history of the Jordan Valley. We have seen from the Biblical story as well as from the story of the potsherds that this place down at the lower end of the Dead Sea, where the doomed cities stood, and where we now sit, had no history from the great catastrophe on down twenty-five hundred years to the Byzantine history here in the East. Thus the return of the captivity of Sodom, the return of fertility in this place, coincides with the beginning of the Dark Ages in Europe. In the turmoil of the centuries that followed, this place was forgotten. At last even Palestine, the Promised Land, was forgotten. This whole region became the realm of the Oriental story-teller.

Then began the re-discovery. Occasional pilgrims, from the seventh century onward, ventured from Christian Europe to the Land of Holy Writ, and left records of their wanderings; they were little more than that. Arculf (A.D. 700) was much interested in the footsteps of our Lord; he ventured into the Jordan Valley at Jericho, but hardly cast a glance down to the location of the Cities of the Plain, or devoted a thought to the history of the fearful event that took place there. One after another, Willibald (721–7), Barnard the Wise

UNSCIENTIFIC SPECULATIONS 109

(867), Seawulf (1102–3), Rabbi Benjamin of Tudela (1160–73), trailed their ways out into various Bible lands, seeking mainly the places to which the memory of the life and work of Christ runs, but seem never to have had a thought for the ancient history of the Patriarchal Period; at least, they left no word of record concerning the Cities of the Plain.

Not until Sir John Maundeville (1322–56), near three thousand years after the days of Abraham and Lot, is there any special interest manifested in this appalling passage of human history. It is indicative of the ultimate perishing of a knowledge of the Orient from the western world that Sir John thought it necessary in his story to give minute descriptions of the way to reach Constantinople, and to pass on from Constantinople to Jerusalem! The legendary character of the good nobleman's account is evident by this extract:

"In that country also, and in some others, are found long apples in their season, which they call apples of Paradise; and they are very sweet and of good savour. And though you cut them in ever so many slices or parts, across or endwise, you will always find in the middle the figure of the holy cross. . . . They find there also the apple tree of Adam, the fruit of which has a bite on one side. And there are also fig-trees which bear no leaves, but figs grow upon the small branches; and men call them figs of Pharoah. Also near Cairo is the field where balm grows: it comes out on small trees, that are no higher than the girdle of a man's breeches, and resemble the wood of the wild vine. And in that field are seven wells, which our Lord Jesus Christ made with one of His feet, when He went to play with other children."[1]

"And a little from Hebron is the mount of Mamre, from which the valley takes its name. And there is an oak tree which the Saracens call *dirpe,* which is of Abraham's time; and people call it the dry tree.... And although it be dry, still it has great virtue; for, certainly, he that hath a little thereof upon him, it heals him of the falling evil, and his horse shall not be afoundered; and many other virtues it hath, on account of which it is highly esteemed."[2]

We are not now surprised to have from him this record concerning the Dead Sea and the Cities of the Plain:

"Neither man, beast, nor anything that hath life, may die in that sea; and that hath been proved many times by men that have been condemned to death, who have been cast therein, and left therein three or four days, and they might never die therein, for it receiveth nothing within him that breatheth life. And no man may drink of the water on account of its bitterness. And if a man cast iron therein, it will float on the surface; but if men cast a feather therein, it will sink to the bottom; and these are things contrary to nature.

"And there beside grow trees that bear apples very fair of color to behold; but when we break or cut them in two we find within ashes and cinders, which is a token that by the wrath of God the cities and the land are burned and sunk into hell. Some call that sea the Lake Dasfetidee; some, the River

[1] *Early Travels in Palestine,* page 152.
[2] *Ibid.,* 162.

UNSCIENTIFIC SPECULATIONS 111

of Devils; and some the river that is ever stinking. Into that sea, by the wrath of God, sunk the five cities, Sodom, Gomorrah, Aldama, Seboym, and Segor, for the abominable sin that reigned in them. But Segor, by the prayer of Lot, was saved and kept a great while, for it was set upon a hill, and some part of it still appears above the water; and men may see the walls when it is fair and clear weather."[3]

Such accounts may provoke an incredulous smile, but for real facts of identification of the location of the Cities of the Plain, they are just about as reliable as the reports of the various travellers and scholars. The great travellers and scholars, Dr. Robinson, Lieutenant Lynch, de Saulcy, Tristram, all down the line to General Kitchener and Professor Huntington, give much valuable information concerning many places, especially along the line of their particular qualifications—Dr. Robinson, Biblical history; Lieutenant Lynch, hydrography; de Saulcy, life in the Orient; Canon Tristram, devotional meditation; Kitchener, military strategy; and Huntington, again hydrography.

But for correct identification of the Cities of the Plain they did practically nothing. As yet the science of Biblical Archaeology in Palestine had not arisen, or was not understood by these distinguished travellers. They use "dead reckoning" of names and local tra-

[3] *Early Travels in Palestine*, page 179.

112 EXPLORATIONS AT SODOM

ditions, which has so often proved so utterly unreliable. Thus it came about that Sodom and Gomorrah have been located at nearly every portion of the Dead Sea, around the whole of the "Great Round." A favourite place has been at the upper end of the Dead Sea where is no trace of the ruins of any city.

Professor Palmer, who did such valuable work of excavation and identification in the Sinai Peninsula, seems to have dropped somewhat his scientific method when he reached the Jordan Valley. He says:

"Writers on sacred topography, from Josephus downwards, have unanimously concurred in assuming the southern portion of the Dead Sea to have been the position of the 'Vale of Siddim' and the 'Cities of the Plain.' Captain Wilson, in an able article upon the site of Ai, shows this view to be erroneous, and I entirely agree with him in placing the site of Sodom and Gomorrah at the northern extremity of the lake. After conclusively proving the identity of Ai with a hill to the east of Bethel 'covered from head to foot with heaps of stones and ruins,' the writer proceeds to discuss the position of the mountain mentioned in Genesis 12:8, where Abraham 'builded an altar to the Lord,' and upon which, as we are told in the next chapter, he agreed to separate from Lot, leaving the latter to choose which portion of the country he would take to dwell in. 'Lot lifted up his eyes and beheld all the plain of the Jordan, that it was well watered everywhere, before the Lord destroyed Sodom and Gomorrah, even as the garden of the Lord, like the land of Egypt, as thou comest to Zoar' (Gen. 13:10). This verse, as Captain Wilson points out, evidently im-

UNSCIENTIFIC SPECULATIONS 113

plies that Lot was actually looking down upon Sodom and Gomorrah at the time; and if, as is expressly stated in the following verse, he journeyed east, this course would have led him away from the southern end of the Dead Sea."[4]

Lieutenant Lynch (1847-8) summarizes his observations in this pious and reassuring comment:

"But it is for the learned to comment on the facts we have laboriously collected. Upon ourselves, the result is a decided one. We entered upon this sea with conflicting opinions. One of the party was skeptical, and another, I think, a professed unbeliever of the Mosaic account. After twenty-two days' close investigation, if I am not mistaken, we are unanimous in the conviction of the truth of the Scriptural account of the destruction of the Cities of the Plain. I record with diffidence the conclusions we have reached, simply as a protest against the shallow deductions of would-be unbelievers."[5]

But as for the location of the cities he has nothing more definite than these words, written in camp while at Jebel Usdum: "Notwithstanding the oppressive heat, there was a pleasure in our strange sensations, lying in the open air, upon the pebbly beach of this desolate and unknown sea, perhaps near the sites of Sodom and Gomorrah; the salt mountains of Usdum in close proximity, and nothing but bright, familiar stars above us."[6] It is

[4] E. H. Palmer, *The Desert of the Exodus*, pages 480-1, Vol. II.
[5] W. F. Lynch, *The River Jordan and the Dead Sea*, p. 380.
[6] W. F. Lynch, *The River Jordan and the Dead Sea*, p. 305.

evident that he favoured this region as the location of the doomed city.

Stanley had much of the spirit of the modern scientific observer, but without the data now possessed. In view of the later discoveries by geologists and explorers, his words seem very penetrating, almost prophetic: "In what precise manner 'the Lord overthrew the cities' is not clearly indicated in the records either of Scripture or of natural remains. The great difference of level between the bottoms of the northern and the southern ends of the lake, the former being a depth of thirteen hundred, the latter only of thirteen feet, below the surface, confirms the theory that the southern end is of recent formation, and, if so, was submerged at the time of the fall of the cities, and that the Vale of Siddim was the whole of the bay south of the promontory which now almost closes up its northern portion."[7]

Canon Tristram found conclusive evidence of the natural fertility of this region.[8]

"All teemed with a prodigality of life. It was, in fact, a reproduction of the oasis of Jericho, in a far more tropical climate, and with yet more lavish supply of water. . . . For three miles we rode through these rich

[7] A. P. Stanley, *Sinai and Palestine*, page 359.
[8] *Land of Israel*, page 336.

groves, revelling in the tropical verdure and swarming ornithology of its labyrinths."

Dr. Robinson [9] with his accustomed acute thinking on all biblical subjects anticipates much of later discovery though some of his explanations miss the mark: "A lake must have existed where the Dead Sea now lies, into which the Jordan poured its waters long before the catastrophe of Sodom. The great depression of the whole broad Jordan Valley and of the northern part of the 'Arabah, the direction of its lateral valleys, as well as the slope of the high western district towards the north, all go to show that the configuration of this region in its main features is coeval with the present condition of the surface of the earth in general, and not the effect of any catastrophe at a subsequent period. In view of the fact of the necessary existence of a lake before the catastrophe of Sodom; the well-watered plain toward the south, in which were the cities of Sodom and Gomorrah, and not far off the sources of bitumen; as also the peculiar character of this part of the lake, where alone asphaltum at the present day makes its appearance—I say, in view of all these facts, there is but a step to the obvious hypothesis, that the fertile plain is now in part occupied by the southern bay lying south of

[9] *Biblical Researches,* ii, 188.

the peninsula; and that, by some convulsion or catastrophe of nature connected with the miraculous destruction of the cities, either the surface of this plain was scooped out, or the bottom of the lake heaved up so as to cause the waters to overflow and cover permanently a larger tract than formerly.''

De Saulcy (1850–1) writes in such an extravagant mood at all times that it is difficult to quote anything as an expression of his real opinion on any definite subject. That he saw some ruins at the place west of Jebel Usdum which he most positively identifies as Sodom and another farther into Judea as Zoar, can hardly be questioned. That they, like the ruined fortress on the Mountains of Moab identified by General Kitchener as Zoar, were only the remains of later guard-houses along the caravan road seems the most likely explanation. That region is about as dry as the Sahara. That the metropolis of the Plain should have been located so far from the water and the fertility is so contrary to commonsense as to be incredible. His identification of Sodom as Kherbet Esdoum seems impossible, though his lively account of his journeys and his spirited argument in favour of his view is most interesting reading.[10]

[10] De Saulcy, *The Dead Sea and the Bible Lands*, Vol. I, Chap. XII.

UNSCIENTIFIC SPECULATIONS 117

Professor Huntington, whose admirable discussion of the climatic changes of Palestine has received deserved attention, was less happy in his attempts at determining the location of the Cities of the Plain. He is quite confident that Sodom was located on the northeastern shore of the Dead Sea above where the River Arnon enters, and is equally confident also that the Dead Sea in the days of Abraham was seventy feet higher than at present.[11]

It seems never to have occurred to this eminent hydrographer and climatologist that if the Sea were seventy feet higher there would be no place for a city at all along the shore; the waters of the Sea would have lapped against the Wall of Moab. He takes no account either in this connection of the filling in of the delta of the Jordan, and the consequent lessening of the evaporating area thus causing the Sea, not to fall seventy feet as he thinks since the days of Abraham, but to rise to a still higher level.

From these ofttimes vague, sometimes foolish, and occasionally contradictory views by travellers and students, it is refreshing to turn to the illuminating observations of the geologists, Wright and Blankenkorn, and now Day,

[11] Ellsworth Huntington, *Palestine and Its Transformation*, 1911.

118 EXPLORATIONS AT SODOM

the geologist of our expedition. The former of these scholars really laid the foundation for scientific work in the geology of this region, and did so almost contemporaneously with the fixing up of the pottery data in Palestine by Petrie. Wright of Oberlin [12] and Blankenkorn,[13] the German geologist, examined this region and reached practically the same conclusions, and these conclusions are carefully examined and corroborated by the geologist of this present expedition, Professor Day of Beirut. The sum of the evidence presented by all these scientists is that this low plain here around about the foot of Jebel Usdum is now a burned-out region of oil and asphalt. It is very interesting on the railroad journey from Kantara, Egypt, to Jerusalem, to note the large iron pipes now lying along the course of the railway, and to learn that these pipes were used by General Allenby to convey water along with the allied army as it went toward Jerusalem, and that they were furnished the army by the Standard Oil Company, and had been imported by them to drill for oil in this very region around Jebel Usdum. The oil has collected again in a subterranean reser-

---

[12] George Frederick Wright, *Scientific Confirmations of Old Testament History*, pp. 118–158.

[13] Dr. Max Blankenkorn, *Zeit. Deutsch. Palestina-Vereins*, Vol. XIX, p. 1.

UNSCIENTIFIC SPECULATIONS 119

voir, or is believed by the scientists of the Company to have done so, and so the matter was about to be tested, when the War stopped all such schemes.

Of this region Emerson,[14] also following the researches of Blankenkorn says: "An old land, cleft at the end of the Tertiary by many faults, between which a great block sank to form the bottom of this deep sea. It carried down in the fossiliferous and gypsum-bearing beds the source of the bitumen and the sulphur. . . . In the earlier portion of this last or post-glacial stadium, a final sinking of a fraction of the bottom of the trough, near the south end of the lake, dissected the low salt plateau, sinking its central parts beneath the salt waters, while fragments remain buttressed against the great walls of the trench forming the plains of Djebel Usdum and the peninsula El Lisan, with the swampy *Sebcha* between. . . . It exposed the wonderful eastern wall of Djebel Usdum: seven miles long, with 30–45 meters of clear blue salt at the base, capped by 125–140 meters of gypsum-bearing marls impregnated with sulphur, and conglomerates at times cemented with bitumen."

Latest of all these scientists is Professor

[14] *Proc. of the A. A. H. S.*, Buffalo, N. Y., 1896, pp. 109–111.

120 EXPLORATIONS AT SODOM

Day, geologist of our Staff: "If Sodom and Gomorrah were, as many think, at the south end of the sea, they may have been shattered by an earthquake, and the ground on which they stood may have been so depressed as to be covered by the waters of the sea. When cities are destroyed by earthquakes, they frequently catch fire, as happened in Japan in 1923. It is also conceivable that the conflagration of Sodom and Gomorrah may have been increased by the ejection of oil or bitumen from the earth. The Vale of Siddim, which is supposed to be the lower part of the 'Arabah near the Dead Sea, is stated to have contained wells of bitumen, 'slime pits.' None is known to exist at the present time. A bitumen spring on the eastern shore, north of the Lisan, was reported to our party, but we did not succeed in reaching the spot to confirm the report. Solid bitumen has been known from ancient times to be thrown upon the shores of the Dead Sea, and it still occurs. It is certainly possible that the Cities of the Plain and the bitumen wells of the Vale of Siddim may be submerged under the shallow waters of the south end of the Dead Sea.

"Volcanic action has sometimes been invoked to explain the catastrophe, but that must be ruled out. There is plenty of eruptive rock in the mountains near the Dead Sea, but it all dates from periods long anterior to the time of man."[15]

We have followed along this bookish digression from the story we are telling that we may see how modern learning has come at last into its own place at the end of a long line of more or less foolish imaginings of pious pilgrims, and equally pious, but more learned Biblical students, who were yet without sufficient data to reach reliable conclusions. From all this we would return now to take up the thread of our Story of Ancient Sodom in the Light of Modern Science.

[15] *Bibliotheca Sacra*, Vol. LXXXI. No. 323, pages 269–270.

V

THE STORY OF ANCIENT SODOM IN THE LIGHT OF MODERN SCIENCE

LETTER TEN:
ON THE DEAD SEA

"OF the catastrophe which destroyed the city and the district of Sodom, we can hardly hope ever to form a satisfactory conception."[1]

"The pottery from Bab-ed-Dra'a is all older than the eighteenth century B.C., at the latest, since none of the characteristic Middle Bronze or Hyksos types appear, and everything is 'first Semitic.' . . . The data we have fixed for the catastrophe of Sodom and Gomorrah, about the early part of the eighteenth century B.C., seems to be exceedingly probable. In any case, there was a great convulsion of nature which destroyed the towns of the Southern Ghor, and made an ineffaceable impression upon the survivors."[2]

[1] George Grove, *Smith's Bible Dictionary*, Ed. 1887, p. 3069.
[2] Dr. W. F. Albright, *The Annual of the American Schools of Oriental Research*, Vol. VI., 1924–5, p. 66.

IN LIGHT OF MODERN SCIENCE 123

These contrasting statements show how great has been the advance in Biblical knowledge in the last fifty years and how absolutely also this advance has been toward the verification of the ancient records. So much for the Light of Modern Science. In fact, as we are now to see in the summing up of the evidence, every item of the story of Sodom and Gomorrah has been certified by scientific evidence.

It is an interesting, though rather tedious, day's ride up from Mezra'ah at El Lisan to the Port of Jericho. Come sit beside me, on the little promenade deck of the old motor-boat, that we may talk over what we have seen. Now that the missing link of evidence has been found, we must put all the links together into a complete chain. Probably many who read these letters have already done this, but others will not have done so. It is always helpful clearly to state conclusions. Some of the evidence in this case is the result of the labors of others, and has been known for many years; some is the result of this expedition. All must be put together for a complete understanding of the case. This is the task before us now.

1. It has been established that there was here a Canaanite civilization of the Early Bronze Age, the time of Abraham and Lot, and of Sodom and Gomorrah, Cities of the

124 EXPLORATIONS AT SODOM

Plain, at the southern end of the Dead Sea, and that this Civilization ceased about the time of Abraham, and was not resumed, nor even succeeded by any other, certainly until the time of Ezekiel, and probably not until Byzantine times. This is the very important conclusion established by the Expedition of Xenia Theological Seminary in coöperation with the American School at Jerusalem to the Cities of the Plain.

The pottery from the graves along the eastern edge of the Plain, the fine old pottery of the Early Bronze Age, together with the primitive Canaanite High Place discovered in connection with these graves, reveals unmistakably the civilization of Palestine at that time. Pieces of bronze were rare and small, a fact pointing to the *beginning* of the Bronze Age, and the same conclusion as to date forces itself on one from the characteristic Early Bronze type of the potsherds. The flint artifacts are naturally contemporaneous with the pottery and bronze; and belong, accordingly, to the so-called aeneolithic period, by definition. During this intermediate period, after the discovery of metal working, men still continued to use some of the stone implements with which they had hitherto been content, though employing copper and an alloy of copper and tin (bronze) for more solid and re-

IN LIGHT OF MODERN SCIENCE 125

sistant instruments. This was the dawn of metallurgy.

This is the first time we have found in Palestine a large station of the early period in the open air and on the surface, with a mixture of flint artifacts, potsherds, and objects of bronze. These finds are similar to those which have been made in the oldest levels of the ancient Canaanite cities so far excavated; Tell el-Hesi (Lachish), Gezer, Megiddo, and especially Tell es-Sultan (Jericho). But there the objects found were buried deep under débris, and the stratification was more or less confused by later foundations and pits, so that one might often be uncertain whether given flints and potsherds were *really contemporaneous*. The station of Bab-ed-Dra'a is thus of extreme importance for the comparative study of the ceramics, flint industry, and bronze culture in the second half of the third millennium.

Then, the careful and painstaking search of the Plain north, south, east, and west, and the examination of ruins down to virgin sand and gravel has failed to reveal any trace of any civilization in twenty-five later centuries. This is negative evidence, it is true; but there are times when negative evidence comes to have all the force of positive evidence, and this is one such instance. For the absolute silence of Scripture concerning any civiliza-

126 EXPLORATIONS AT SODOM

tion on this Plain from the time of Abraham onward, certainly to the time of Ezekiel, and most probably to the end of the period of Old Testament revelation, finds its counterpart and confirmation in this like silence in the testimony of the ruins on the Plain, in the period during which the prophets cited the condition of Sodom as a warning. Thus science and revelation tell here the same story.

2. The next thing in order concerning this Plain is that the only correct description of the natural conditions of life here is that given in the Bible, "Even as the Garden of the Lord, before the Lord destroyed Sodom and Gomorrah." It is quite easy to realize as we sit on the deck of our motor-boat in the boiling sun of March what the heat on the Plain must be in July. But it is so in many places in the tropics. Heat and cold are comparative terms to express climatic conditions. Natives of India have been known to perish of cold when caught out over night in time of light frost. We would doubtless find the summer heat on the Plain intolerable, yet it means tropical luxuriousness. Altogether, now that the captivity of Sodom has been restored, and climatic action has fully washed out the salt and sulphur from the Plain, the only correct description of the natural conditions of life on the

IN LIGHT OF MODERN SCIENCE 127

Plain is in fact as set out in the words of Scripture, "Like the Garden of the Lord."

3. Having verified the Canaanite civilization on the Plain for the time of Abraham and Lot and having discovered the natural conditions of life there, now that the effects of the great tragedy have passed away, we come to the heart of the Story of Ancient Sodom in the Light of Modern Science; the great catastrophe did take place exactly as narrated in the Bible. We are just now passing Messada there on the left and coming toward the gorge at the mouth of the Arnon there on the right, while the sugar-loaf of Jebel Usdum is sinking to the horizon yonder in the South. It is a favourable occasion for a careful survey of all the evidence of that tragedy.

The Biblical story is from the standpoint of divine Providence; it draws aside the curtain to let us see what God was doing. Science examines only the remaining evidence of what happened, what the geologists are able to tell us of the natural remains of what took place: the Biblical writers tell of the divine agency; the geologists know the effects. This expedition only collated and confirmed this evidence.

According to the Biblical story the Plain and all the inhabitants of it and all that grew out of the ground were destroyed by a rain of fire and brimstone from heaven. The account indicates also that salt was mixed with the descending fiery rain; one of the refugees, like some of those at Pompeii, tarried too much and was caught in the descending deluge and incrusted with salt, as indeed the mountain peaks near by are to this day. Thus the whole region was ruined and rendered uninhabitable for two millenniums and more. The Biblical account shows how the timing of the events was entirely in the hands of God which held the fire in leash till Lot be gotten out. It is also made known that a vast column of smoke, as from a furnace up to heaven, was seen by Abraham from far-off Hebron. So far the Bible.

But the Biblical account does not tell us the original source of the sulphur and the salt, whether natural or supernatural, though these elements as finished products are set forth here in the event as real salt and sulphur. Nor does the Bible say how they came to be up in the sky, or what kindled the fire, or caused the smoke. Concerning all these things we must turn to the findings of the geologists from their examination of things as they are on the Plain.

This region was found by the geologists to be a burned-out region of oil and asphalt, of

IN LIGHT OF MODERN SCIENCE 129

which material, indeed, there is again an accumulation that will soon be exploited, even now, as I write, such exploitation is being reported. Now wherever these conditions exist there is an accumulation of gases, and the geologists tell us that here, at some time which they cannot exactly fix, these gases were ignited by some means, also to them unknown, and there was a great explosion, with first an upheaval, and then a subsidence of the strata.

The character of the ruptured strata has also been determined, with most interesting conclusions. There is along the lower part of this Plain a great stratum of rock salt, which on the western side of the Plain shows itself in that great salt mountain, now known as Jebel Usdum. At its base is a stratum of rock salt about one hundred and fifty feet thick. It is almost pure salt, but lies in layers of varying thickness. Mixed with the layers of salt, and falling down over them also, is a marl in which is much free sulphur, lumps of which we picked up along the sea. When the explosion of the gases took place, this stratum of salt mixed with sulphur was ruptured with the other strata, and the salt and sulphur carried up into the heavens red-hot, and so rained down upon Sodom and Gomorrah and over the whole region, exactly as the Scripture de-

130 EXPLORATIONS AT SODOM

scribes the rain of fire and brimstone from heaven. Mixed with the salt and sulphur was also the asphalt, heated to a high degree.

Now, what makes a greater smoke than a vat of boiling asphalt at work on the street? Thus we have an exact accounting for the smoke up to heaven, "as the smoke of a furnace." A low place in the hills toward Hebron opened the way for Abraham to see this distinctly from that distant point.

Thus the geologists have found in nature exactly what the Biblical record describes in Providence. The sacred writer draws aside the veil and lets us see the immediate working of the hand of God; the geologist looks upon the materials upon which the hand of God was employed, and shows us what was done. We have thus a scientific account of the miracle, and at the same time its confirmation. Thus, while only in the Bible do we get an explanation of the events, science is able to certify that the events took place.

4. The exact location of the Cities of the Plain must next be considered. We are obliged to report that none of the places heretofore pointed out as the site of any one of the Cities of the Plain is in fact so. The archaeological evidence, the pottery of the Early Bronze Age, is not found at any of these places. They largely represent the work of the Crusaders,

as at el Ubrous, thought by General Kitchener to be ancient Zoar, still more the work of Arab times early and late, and in small part Byzantine work at a time when there was a bishopric at Zoar.

The treatment of this subject is necessarily different from that of those phases of the story already considered. The ruins of the houses have not certainly been seen by any one in modern times. The location of the Cities is determined by a process of deductive logic. Today, however, inductive reasoning is most in favour, because in the past deductive reasoning has too often been upon *a priori* premises, hence the result something of an assumption. But deductive reasoning is satisfactory, provided the premises are established by an induction of facts. In such case deductive logic is stronger in its conclusion than inductive reasoning, because the conclusion is drawn not from one set of facts only, but from two or more sets of facts according to the dependable laws of formal logic.

In this case of the location of the Cities, the premises are established as facts beyond reasonable cavil. The major premise is that certainly the catastrophe took place where the ruins of the catastrophe now are; ruins do not move around; place-names and local traditions may move even long distances, but ruins stay put. Now the ruins of the catastrophe, and, indeed, all the remaining undisturbed materials, are right here at Jebel Usdum. Here is the stratum of rock-salt, here the overlying marl mixed with free sulphur, and the whole region round about attests the disruptive character of some event that scattered the salt and the sulphur far and wide, incrusted the mountain peaks, and so blasted the earth that it took twenty-five hundred years of climatic influences to wash out the soil and make the Plain again "as the Garden of the Lord."

The minor premise consists of a number of facts established by observation and investigation. Moab lies to the east; into that land Lot escaped, when he became afraid to remain any longer even in Zoar. Thus Sodom and Gomorrah must have been well to the western side of the narrow Plain, since Zoar seemed a safe place of refuge. This puts the doomed cities near Jebel Usdum.

Then the rivers that come into the lower end of the Sea from the mountains converge toward a point immediately in front of Jebel Usdum. A small boy announced to his father that he had discovered a wonderful arrangement of Providence that always made a river run by a great city! Our camp and the camp of the soldiers on the Plain lay by the streams.

IN LIGHT OF MODERN SCIENCE 133

Bedouin villages were similarly located. Every ruin on the Plain has been so located. Water is a human necessity and Oriental cities went to the water rather than brought the water to themselves. At the confluence of these rivers, as indeed, the world over, we may expect the metropolis of the Plain; so again, in front of Jebel Usdum.

In seeking the exact location of the Cities of the Plain, we must take particular notice of the fact that in the days of Abraham the Sea was at a much lower level than it now is. We have seen from the description of the researches, especially of the shallow water and the submerged forest, that a lower level of water would mean a larger extent of the Plain. How much larger, however, does not appear until we have taken particular notice of other evidence already before us, some before us even for a long time. The geologists have shown that in geological ages the Sea was at a much higher level. This fact naturally raises the question, Was the Sea at any time at a lower level than now?

The immediate answer is already before us. The submerged forest shows conclusively that fifty years ago the Sea was at a much lower level, and the fact that the water has reached the higher ground all around the Sea makes it certain that it will continue to rise for a

134   EXPLORATIONS AT SODOM

long time yet, *if there is anything to cause a demand for increase in the surface of the Sea.*

There is now, and has been in all ages, just such a demand. If sand or gravel is put in the edge of a basin of water, either the water will rise in the basin or it will run over the edge. It will not rise—if it can run over the edge—until the place into which it runs over is filled up to the level of the water in the basin. The Dead Sea is just such a basin. The Jordan River brings down enormous quantities of detritus and fills in a great delta at the northern end of the Sea. Since the days of Joshua it has filled in the Sea from Beth Hogla down to the present shore line, a distance of nearly six miles, or almost one-seventh of the deep part of the Sea.

The problem of nature at such a sea is the problem of an equilibrium between inflow and evaporation. If the inflow is greater than the evaporation, the Sea rises until it can run over the edge and increase the evaporating area. The filling in of the Jordan delta caused exactly this to be done. As the evaporating area was greater in the days of Abraham, when the Sea extended to Beth Hogla, the Sea was then lower than now, and as it filled in, it rose until it could run over the edge. It could not run over the eastern edge, for there is the Wall of

IN LIGHT OF MODERN SCIENCE 135

Moab. It could not run over the western edge, for there are the mountains of Judea. It could not run over the upper end of the Sea for that is up stream. The only edge low enough to run over is the edge toward this Plain at the lower end of the Sea. It had not run over here when the Roman road came down to the end of the Lisan to cross over; it had not entirely done so even seventy-five years ago, at which time these Kerak Arabs remember the ford at the lower end of the Sea. Latterly it has risen rapidly, and covered nearly the whole Plain with shallow water. Thirty-five years ago, when I first saw the Sea, it was so much lower than now that there was a beautiful island in the north end of the Sea, but today, as we approach the Port of Jericho we pass over the region of that island in several feet of water.

One other subject connected with the Cities of the Plain is still to be considered in this summing up of scientific evidence. Lot is called the father of Moab which, of course, does not mean that every inhabitant of Moab was a lineal descendant of Lot any more than it is implied that every American is a lineal descendant from Washington, when he is called the father of his country. Lot was the progenitor of Moabite civilization. His two sons became leaders of two political parties which

136 EXPLORATIONS AT SODOM

ultimately resulted in the two separate states, Moab and Ammon. This civilization of Moab is also represented in the Pentateuch to have attained a high degree at Kir of Moab in the days of Moses. It is quite possible now to test both this *terminus a quo* and this *terminus ad quem* of Moabite civilization, the point from which it started in the days of Abraham and Lot, and the stage which it reached in the time of Moses.

In front of the temple of Luxor there stands the base of a statue of Rameses the Great, which I uncovered in 1908. Around the base of this statue is a line of inscriptions giving the names of peoples whom the Pharaoh boasted as having been conquered by himself or his predecessors. In this list is Moab, spelled out in hieroglyphic characters as plainly and unmistakably as in letters in our English Bible. Thus a little before the Exodus, Moab, far away across the Sinai peninsula from Egypt, was of sufficient importance to be the subject of a boastful inscription by Rameses the Great. This confirms the statement in the Pentateuch concerning Moses at Kir of Moab.

We desired also to get the material evidence in the ruins of Kerak of these same events. For some days as recounted in the story of our researches, we did not find it, until at last

IN LIGHT OF MODERN SCIENCE 137

our geologist found the ancient pottery on the precipice east of town. Now the pottery here was not the pottery of the time of Lot and Abraham, but the pottery of the Early Iron Age or the end of the Late Bronze Age, exactly the time when Moses led the Israelites through this region.

It is not so easy to determine the *terminus a quo* of Moabite civilization, the Abramic civilization from which it purports to have started. Moab is a large territory. It was impossible that we could explore all of it, so that the evidence has not been exhausted. It is thus impossible to say yet that evidence of an earlier civilization than that of the time of Lot may not appear. It has not yet appeared.

We did, however, examine the region immediately above where the Cities of the Plain were located. There an old Moabite temple was discovered at Adar, the only Moabite temple yet known. It lies immediately above the Plain, and the pottery showed nothing earlier than the end of the Early Bronze, and the beginning of the Middle Bronze Age, a transition period, which exactly corresponds to the representation of the Bible that Moabite civilization began with Lot's flight from Zoar.

The story of ancient Sodom in the light of modern science is thus a very complete and satisfactory story. Every item of it is certified in regular order.

1. The civilization of the days of Abraham which the Bible represents to have been on the Plain at that time is found to have been actually there and the absence of any trace of civilization of any kind from that time down to A.D. 600, is in exact accord with the silence of Biblical history concerning this Plain from the destruction of the city to the end of the history.

2. The natural conditions of life on the plain also as described in the account in Genesis are exactly confirmed today; "like the garden of the Lord, before the Lord destroyed Sodom and Gomorrah."

3. The great catastrophe described in the Bible did actually take place.

4. The cities are clearly shown to have stood in front of Jebel Usdum where they lie under the waters today. The High Place of the Plain, clearly a place of great importance, as shown by the fortifications, is now well known.

5. And last of all, the evidence makes it quite possible that Lot should be the progenitor of Moabite civilization, which certainly had attained considerable importance by the time Moses passed by the old Kir of Moab.

VI

CONCLUSION: THE PORT OF JERICHO

LETTER ELEVEN:
THE PORT OF JERICHO

THE shadow of the Judean hills has fallen over us with welcome relief from this boiling Dead Sea sun. The wall of Moab on the east is etched in that bold relief that a clear sunset always gives that picturesque coast. Our clumsy craft slowly approaches the wharf at the Port of Jericho, and the automobile appears that gives immediate hope of Jerusalem and supper and loved ones. As we look back over the waters to the region of the Cities of the Plain our discoveries there are seen in their true perspective.

Thus the Story of Ancient Sodom in the Light of Modern Science adds another instance to a long and ever growing list of evidences of the trustworthiness of ancient documents, and especially the ancient documents of Holy Writ. Criticism and archaeology have been proceeding along parallel lines in Bible Lands. A destructive criticism has started from the untrustworthiness of ancient documents to essay the task of rewriting the documents and reconstructing the history of Israel. Archaeology is proceeding along a parallel line, but in the opposite direction, toward the trustworthiness of ancient documents, and with ever-accumulating evidence.

Professor Ernest Sellin of the Berlin University in a recent *brochure* (The Aftermath Series, Number 6, *Archaeology versus Wellhausenism*, edited by Bishop Horace M. Du Bose, D.D.) surveys this accumulating evidence and concludes thus: "If I rightly understand our time, and especially the modern science of the Old Testament, the era of Wellhausen, in spite of all that we have learned of him, may be considered, with us in Germany, as antiquated and wholly of the past. This I deem to be proven by the generation of scholars growing up among us, who, both in respect of science and religion, are thinking from categories quite different from those of the time of Wellhausen." These scholars to whom Sellin refers are expressing themselves in similar vein. Indeed, the whole trend of German and Dutch archaeological scholarship is in this direction. British and American scholarship is following rather slowly.

But archaeological research is progressing

CONCLUSION 141

rapidly and, when the trustworthiness of Scripture is finally and completely established, any theory based upon the untrustworthiness of the ancient documents will come down like a house of cards. *Facts are final.*

www.ingramcontent.com/pod-product-compliance
Lightning Source LLC
Chambersburg PA
CBHW070916160426
43193CB00011B/1488